Judith Schley

summer 2018

EXPERIENCING BIG BAND JAZZ

The Listener's Companion
Gregg Akkerman, Series Editor

Titles in **The Listener's Companion** provide readers with a deeper understanding of key musical genres and the work of major artists and composers. Aimed at nonspecialists, each volume explains in clear and accessible language how to *listen* to works from particular artists, composers, and genres. Looking at both the context in which the music first appeared and has since been heard, authors explore with readers the environments in which key musical works were written and performed.

EXPERIENCING BIG BAND JAZZ

A Listener's Companion

Jeff Sultanof

ROWMAN & LITTLEFIELD
Lanham • Boulder • New York • London

Published by Rowman & Littlefield
A wholly owned subsidiary of The Rowman & Littlefield Publishing Group,
Inc.
4501 Forbes Boulevard, Suite 200, Lanham, Maryland 20706
www.rowman.com

Unit A, Whitacre Mews, 26-34 Stannary Street, London SE11 4AB

British Library Cataloguing in Publication Information Available

Library of Congress Cataloging-in-Publication Data

Names: Sultanof, Jeff.
Title: Experiencing big band jazz : a listener's companion / Jeff Sultanof.
Description: Lanham : Rowman & Littlefield, [2017] | Series: The listener's companion | Includes
    bibliographical references and index.
Identifiers: LCCN 2017020548 (print) | LCCN 2017020728 (ebook) | ISBN 9781442242432 (elec-
    tronic) | ISBN 9781442242425 (cloth : alk. paper)
Subjects: LCSH: Big band music—History and criticism
Classification: LCC ML3518 (ebook) | LCC ML3518 .S84 2017 (print) | DDC 784.4/8165—dc23
    LC record available at https://lccn.loc.gov/2017020548

∞ ™ The paper used in this publication meets the minimum requirements of
American National Standard for Information Sciences Permanence of Paper
for Printed Library Materials, ANSI/NISO Z39.48-1992.

Printed in the United States of America

To Richard Sudhalter,
who told me that I should be writing books

Also to Susan and Alex

CONTENTS

SERIES EDITOR'S FOREWORD

The goal of the Listener's Companion series is to give readers a deeper understanding of pivotal musical genres and the creative work of their iconic composers and performers. This is accomplished in an inclusive manner that does not necessitate extensive music training or elitist shoulder rubbing. Authors of the series place the reader in specific listening experiences in which the music is examined in its historical context with regard to both compositional and societal parameters. By positioning the reader in the real or supposed environment of the music's creation, the author provides for a deeper enjoyment and appreciation of the art form. Series authors, often drawing on their own expertise as both performers and scholars, deliver to readers a broad understanding of major musical genres and the achievements of artists within those genres as lived listening experiences.

"Big band jazz" is an enormous and difficult topic to present in the Listener's Companion series. The murky origins of the genre with blues, "sweet music," and show tunes are not always agreed upon. Terminology is tricky for the uninitiated with aspects like "swing feel" and improvisation playing key roles. And throughout it all rumbles the issue of race and social context. For decades the term *jazz* was related to the "other," or more blatantly, "those folks across the tracks." As a young fan and student of jazz in the 1970s and 1980s, I was a member of the "stage band" at public school. Even in those "modern" times, using the word *jazz* to describe a performance group was not considered safe in America's education system. When I asked my neighborhood piano teacher if I could perform jazz, I was presented either Joplin's ragtime staple "The Entertainer" or the theme from *The Pink Panther* as acceptably inoffensive choices—neither (I learned much later) truly representative of the jazz idiom. Yet the very essence of contemporary pop music can trace its heritage to elements first explored and enjoyed during the age of the big bands. Dancing as a statement of youth culture, the recording industry striving to present the next big thing, dress styles and slang, and the cult of personality: all this and more was happening in the 1930s just as it is today, and it serves as a fabulous mechanism to understand where American music might develop in the future.

Fortunately, the Listener's Companion series has Jeff Sultanof to walk us through the century-long history of big band jazz with the emphasis always being the experience of how the music sounded in the context of its time and how it sounds today. Sultanof combines his extensive background as an editor, arranger, composer, and educator to present a highly engaging narrative that walks the reader through the origins of the big band genre right up to the latest forays of contemporary jazz ensembles, and he does so in a conversational style that appeals to both the studied musician and nonperforming enthusiast. As series editor, I am overjoyed to see one of America's great twentieth-century genres represented so eloquently by Jeff Sultanof.

Gregg Akkerman

ACKNOWLEDGMENTS

The staff at Rowman & Littlefield has been wonderful to work with. I thank Bennett Graff, Gregg Akkerman, Natalie Mandziuk, Kathleen O'brien, and Darren Williams for bringing this information to printed and electronic life.

I am in debt to the Institute of Jazz Studies and the friendship of Dan Morgenstern, Vincent Pelote, Elizabeth Surles, and the late Ed Berger, John Clement, and Anne Kuebler. Their counsel has always been beneficial and has led me down many marvelous roads of discovery.

I am also in debt to Rob and Doug DuBoff, who honor me by publishing editions of classic big band and vocal/orchestra music, which I assist in editing.

Many thanks to the staff of the Institute of Audio Research and to my wonderful students.

INTRODUCTION

Welcome to *Experiencing Big Band Jazz: A Listener's Companion*. This volume is a guide to one of the most creative sources of jazz and popular music since the early twentieth century.

To begin, let's use the newspaper reporter format to furnish a quick background of the subject matter explored in this book.

What: Big bands were created as ensembles that provided music for dancing. Arrangements of new pop songs were written by skilled musicians called "arrangers" for the bands to play. Those that became hits were then requested by dancers. There were also original compositions played and danced to. Full ensemble sounds were often contrasted and enhanced by improvised solos. Some big bands later evolved into concert ensembles and became a new medium for composers.

Who: Leaders and members of ensembles became as popular as Hollywood stars, and thousands of musicians were employed to play in bands with massed reeds, brass, and rhythm sections. Some units even had string sections.

Where: Even though the big band is considered an ensemble made in America, such bands played for dancing all over Canada, Latin America, and Europe.

How: Bands performed in ballrooms and hotels, on recordings, on sponsored radio (and later television) shows, and live broadcasts from places where they were appearing. They were also seen in movies, either incorporated into the plot or showcased in short films.

Speaking of those broadcasts, thousands of hours of live music were preserved by radio networks, the U.S. government, and die-hard fans. Many of these priceless performances have gotten into circulation and are widely available. When possible, recordings cited are from live broadcasts and videos, as we get a better sense of how bands sounded when they performed in front of the public.

Bands came in all sizes and colors: white, black, and various shades of Latin American and Cuban. Some played music that was corny even back then; some had gimmicks. Other bands were the backdrop for a star vocalist or instrumental soloist. In this book, we concentrate on the recordings of bands playing hot swing and jazz. Some ensembles played jazz more than others, and some are hard to categorize. Any dance band was expected to play all sorts of music if requested. Fletcher Henderson led one of the premiere hot dance ensembles of the 1920s, but his was also a house band at Roseland, one of the most well-known ballrooms in America, and it was required to play waltzes and tangos, for a time with Louis Armstrong supplying most of the cornet solos. Jimmie Lunceford led one of the hottest bands on the planet, and yet he played waltzes as well, as did Benny Goodman, who even recorded one!

Of the many hundreds of ensembles, those that appear in the main text were carefully selected for their place in history and musical content, so there is a listing for additional listening. This book is only the beginning; big bands that played jazz have been with us in one form or another since about 1920, and there are hundreds of individual recordings and albums that should be heard. This book is meant to guide the reader for a long time, and with this background, further exploration is encouraged, one ensemble leading to another.

The neat thing is that you don't have to spend one penny to listen to the examples cited in this book; all but one of them discussed in this book are on the Web via YouTube or Spotify. At one time hard to obtain, now even the rarest of recordings are in circulation and relatively easy to hear.

The first chapter of this book sets the stage for the early days of jazz to provide background for the coverage of the first big bands. There have been important discoveries made by me and my colleagues doing first- and secondhand research in popular music, causing a major re-evaluation of the early years of jazz and swing. I am indebted to them for inviting me to question and explore.

The second chapter describes the first flowering of the dance orchestra during the 1920s and how the managerial and booking structures were created for these ensembles.

Chapter 3 starts off with the music heard during the Depression, when jazz was on hiatus as far as most of the public was concerned, but discusses some of the jazz activity that took place.

Chapter 4 explodes with the beginnings of the swing era, as a new generation of listeners embraced the music of Benny Goodman, Tommy Dorsey, and Glenn Miller. I write about the devastating two-year ban of most instrumental recordings in the United States, as well as the impact of World War II on the popular music front. By the end of the decade (covered in chapter 6), the bands were still a voice in American music, but many were disbanding and listeners had moved on to star vocalists such as Frank Sinatra.

From the 1950s on, big bands were still touring, but ballrooms were closing and television became the free entertainment of choice for most, although bands continued to broadcast. Excellent ensembles were put together for recording studio–only projects, and these ensembles are also found in these pages. Rehearsal bands could be found playing on Monday nights at many places throughout the world, and many excellent ensembles got their starts playing such gigs, recording, and even some touring. This continues as these words are written.

I discovered big bands from original copies of recordings and read George T. Simon's important 1966 book on the subject, which was the starting point for most music historians, arrangers, and big band enthusiasts born after 1950. I sought out the written music to study it and have examined thousands of pages of original scores and parts that the musicians actually played so that this music could be properly edited and published. I humbly state that I am a pioneer in this field and am gratified that much of the music you read about here can now be performed, studied, and treasured by musicians and fans all over the globe. A place to find this music may be found at the end of this book in "Recorded Sources and Further Listening."

The big band continues to be a source of great music in many genres and provides yet another medium for the creative expression of composers, arrangers, and improvisers. This book celebrates those pioneers who created and fostered the new popular music of the twentieth century, up to and including the many composer/leaders of today's bands.

It was written to provide a contemporary profile of this wonderful genre for new listeners and scholars alike. I am honored to be your tour guide.

DEFINING OUR TURF

The earliest big bands were made up of about eight or nine musicians, with at least two saxophones, two trumpets, a trombone, a guitar or banjo, piano, string or brass bass (tuba or bass saxophone), and drums, although in the years before electrical recording (the mid-1920s), a full drum set could not be recorded, and the drummer used a woodblock or something else to keep the pulse. This was the instrumentation of several ensembles in the 1920s, but a few were quite large and even had string sections.

By the 1940s, some big bands featured unusual instrumentation (there was a band that was made up of all reeds). By the time the vocalists had taken over the popular music scene, and the music lover was buying long play records in addition to single records, recording dates featured ensembles of all instrumental types, which could still be thought of as big bands. This book includes some of these unusual groundbreaking ensembles that never performed outside of a recording studio, with the accent on jazz composition and improvisation. This also gives us the opportunity to include smaller big bands.

If you are reading these words, the big band may be new to you, or perhaps you are playing in a big band in high school or college. It is my hope that when you are through, you'll be aware of the limitless possibilities offered by this ensemble and you'll appreciate why big bands will never go away.

Note: This book was written to be read two ways: from cover to cover, and jumping around to explore specific bands and/or eras. Whichever way you use this volume, enjoy your musical travels.

TIMELINE

1800s   The earliest "named" dance orchestras are formed and play for formal occasions; leaders include Joseph Lanner and Johann Strauss. In the United States, Francis Johnson becomes one of the first leaders to attain success.

1890s   Introduction of ragtime, primarily played by pianists, but later performed by concert bands.

1900s   African American sideshow and tent show bands are heard playing ragtime and syncopated music.

          A new style of music is first heard in New Orleans that would later become known as jazz.

1910s   The word *jazz* first appears in print as a sports term and later refers to the new syncopated music heard all over the country in vaudeville.

1913   James Reese Europe's musicians play for Vernon and Irene Castle, the top dance team in the country. Europe becomes their musical director and makes recordings for the Victor Talking Machine Company.

1919   Art Hickman's Orchestra makes recordings for the Columbia Graphophone Company.

1920   Paul Whiteman begins recording for the Victor Talking Machine Company. He would become the most prominent bandleader of the first American big band era, selling millions of records.

1924   Louis Armstrong joins the Fletcher Henderson Orchestra, one of the resident dance orchestras at Roseland, perhaps the most renowned ballroom in the United States. His exciting improvisational style influences the entire Henderson Orchestra, and musicians come to hear and learn from him.

Music Corporation of America (MCA) is formed, the first large booking agency for big bands.

1927   Duke Ellington's Orchestra opens at the Cotton Club, and his frequent broadcasts are heard nationwide.

1930   Ensembles disband because of the Depression. Many of the musicians join radio orchestras.

1934   Benny Goodman's Orchestra plays on the "Let's Dance" program, introducing swing music to a national audience. Fletcher Henderson becomes one of his arrangers.

1935   Tommy Dorsey leaves the orchestra he coleads with his brother Jimmy and forms his own. His orchestra would be called the most versatile big band in history.

1936   Count Basie's orchestra is a big hit in Chicago and begins recording for Decca Records.

1938   The Benny Goodman Orchestra plays a concert at Carnegie Hall, the first swing orchestra to do so.

1939   Glenn Miller has a huge hit with "In the Mood," which becomes the anthem of the swing era.

1940   Artie Shaw returns from an extended vacation, records "Frenesi," and reorganizes a new orchestra with strings. Harry James and Tommy Dorsey add string sections soon after.

1941   The Stan Kenton Orchestra plays its first major gig in California. It would perform, record, and tour off and on until 1978. Kenton introduces many musicians who become legendary and commissions music from some of the most important composers of the twentieth century.

1942   James Caesar Petrillo calls for all union musicians to cease recording if record labels do not pay monies to a performance fund, insisting that broadcasts of recordings diminish live music opportunities. Decca and Capitol settle with the union in 1943; Columbia and Victor hold out until 1944.

Glenn Miller disbands, volunteers for army duty, and forms one of the greatest popular music orchestras in history. Robert Farnon, Sam Donahue, and George Melachrino also lead excellent service bands.

1943   Duke Ellington plays his first Carnegie Hall concert and premieres the three-movement "Black, Brown and Beige." He plays Carnegie Hall many times, usually introducing a new concert work.

1944   Because of the draft, the recording ban, rationing, and entertainment taxes, big bands are no longer the focus of the popular music scene. Such singers as Frank Sinatra, Dinah Shore, and Dick Haymes are now the national music favorites.

1946   Benny Goodman and Les Brown disband. Although they later reorganize, many historians consider this the end of the big band era.

The new small-group jazz style named "bebop" is now part of the repertoire of big bands. The Dizzy Gillespie and Gerald Wilson orchestras are very successful.

Claude Thornhill reorganizes his orchestra with the innovative Gil Evans as musical director.

1947   Jimmie Lunceford, the leader of one of the most exciting big bands of the era, dies while on the road.

Machito and His Afro-Cubans introduce a jazz-flavored Cuban style of music later called "cubop." Charlie Parker, Howard McGhee, and Flip Philips make recordings and live appearances with the orchestra.

1948   Recordings by the Ted Heath Orchestra of the United Kingdom are released in the United States by London

Records. His is considered one of the greatest big bands of all time.

The success of Les Brown's recording of "I've Got My Love to Keep Me Warm" proves that big bands can still produce hit records.

1951   Quincy Jones joins the Lionel Hampton Orchestra as a trumpet player/arranger. He leads a successful big band of his own some years later and would later become a vice president of Mercury Records.

1952   Forced to disband in 1949, Count Basie now reorganizes a new band. Many of the musicians become jazz legends.

Eddie Sauter and Bill Finegan form an orchestra that would become one of the legendary ensembles of all time featuring reeds and percussion of all types, proving once again that challenging music could sell records. It disbands in 1957.

1953   Shorty Rogers orchestrates Leith Stevens's score for *The Wild One*, which is recorded by an all-star ensemble of top jazz session musicians. It's one of the earliest examples of jazz used in a motion picture score.

1956   Stan Kenton records Johnny Richards's *Cuban Fire*, later cited as one of the finest examples of the fusion of big band jazz and Cuban music.

Recording studios now use two- and three-track recorders for sessions in stereophonic sound. In 1958, the stereo LP is introduced, opening up greater sonic possibilities for large ensembles.

Duke Ellington plays "Diminuendo and Crescendo in Blue" and causes a near-riot at the Newport Jazz Festival. He and his band become more popular than ever.

1959   John Dankworth's U.K. ensemble is a big hit at the Newport Jazz Festival.

1966   Thad Jones and Mel Lewis put together a band to play a few Monday nights at the Village Vanguard. The ensemble still plays on Monday nights and is known as the Vanguard Jazz Orchestra.

Don Ellis's ensemble is a surprise hit at the Monterey Jazz Festival, playing a repertoire influenced by rock and ethnic music in unusual meters. It attracts audiences of all age groups and even plays rock clubs and concerts.

Drummer Buddy Rich organizes a band and publicizes it on *The Tonight Show Starring Johnny Carson*. Most of the musicians are recent college grads.

1967   Paul Whiteman dies.

1968   Trombonist/composer Rob McConnell puts together a brass ensemble to record pop songs called the Boss Brass. He later adds saxophones and turns it into a standard big band. One of the finest big bands in the world, McConnell drops the format and leads a ten-piece ensemble in 2000.

1969   South African pianist/composer Chris McGregor forms the Brotherhood of Breath. It attracts large crowds in Europe, but audience support is never large enough to sustain it. McGregor dies in 1990.

1971   Louis Armstrong dies.

1975   The National Jazz Ensemble directed by Chuck Israels makes the first of two albums. The multigenerational ensemble performs music from the 1920s through the 1970s. It becomes the model for future repertory orchestras such as the American Jazz Orchestra, the New York Jazz Repertory Ensemble, and Jazz at Lincoln Center.

1986   Benny Goodman dies.

2000   Sierra Music publishes new editions of the repertoire of the Stan Kenton and Maynard Ferguson orchestras.

Rob and Doug DuBoff found ejazzlines as a distributor for jazz products, but soon form Jazz Lines Publications to make available edited, corrected editions of classic big band music from the 1920s through the present time. By 2017, they have hundreds of titles in print from a variety of bands and singers from authentic sources. Big bands throughout the world embrace these publications, and they are used in university courses at the masters and doctoral levels.

SOME TECHNICAL TERMS

When reading about music, and specifically the big bands, some ideas and concepts should be introduced before beginning our journey.

INSTRUMENTATION

Big bands were usually composed of the following instruments:

Reeds and Woodwinds

Most bands had alto, tenor, and later baritone saxophones. During the 1920s, some bands had soprano and bass saxophones. Large ensembles such as the Paul Whiteman band had the small sopranino sax (in fact, it is present in the original version of George Gershwin's "Rhapsody in Blue").

The B♭ clarinet was a required double for reed players, and all saxophonists played the instrument; baritone saxophonists usually doubled on bass clarinet.

Other woodwinds often featured were flute, oboe, and bassoon. Some musicians played an unusual instrument during the 1920s called a Couesnophone (or "goofus"), a saxophone-shaped instrument with a keyboard similar to a modern-day melodica.

The 1950s Sauter-Finegan Orchestra also featured toy trumpets and kazoos.

Brass

Trumpets were usually played in big bands, but cornets were used as well during the 1920s, as well as mellophones, instruments that looked like French horns with the bell facing outward. Later in the 1960s, the flugelhorn became an instrument of choice for arrangers, as it blended with reeds beautifully and created a large, warm sound.

Trombones were the slide variety most of the time, but musicians such as Juan Tizol (Ellington band) and Bob Brookmeyer (Thad Jones-Mel Lewis) played the valve trombone.

Brass instrumentalists continue to use a variety of mutes, which are put over or into the bell of the instrument. Straight mutes, cup mutes, plungers (the same as a "plumber's helper") and Harmon mutes are mentioned in the text.

Strings

Many bands had string sections during the 1920s and after 1940. In fact, saxophone players often doubled on violin.

Rhythm Instruments

The banjo would usually be found in big bands in the 1920s, but the guitar was the instrument of choice by the end of the decade.

The tuba was used extensively as a rhythm instrument to reinforce the left hand of the piano in the 1920s. String basses became the norm by 1935, although the tuba was still used as part of the brass section in some bands.

Piano and drum set completed the ensemble. Drum sets could be extensive, with bells, chimes, vibraphone, and even gongs as part of a percussionist's arsenal of sound.

AABA SONG FORM

Since we are dealing with popular songs in this book, it's important to understand the form of most songs since they are referenced throughout. The song proper is usually called a refrain, and the form you most often see is AABA.

This means that the first strain (or melodic phrase) is usually repeated. The B section is usually called the "bridge" and is a different melodic phrase. The A section returns to complete the song.

As an example, let's take a song like "Over the Rainbow." The phrase that starts "Somewhere . . ." is played and sung twice (AA), the bridge begins with "Someday I'll wish . . ," (B) and the song ends with another melodic statement of "Somewhere . . ."(A).

Several songs had verses, which served as introductions to the songs themselves; this was a way of introducing the song, particularly if it was written for a Broadway show. Some of these verses sound like complete songs in their own right, and in a couple of instances, verses have been recorded without the refrain (one example: Frank Sinatra recorded the verse to "Stardust" without the refrain in 1962). In several of the big band recordings from the 1920s in particular, the verse was performed after the first AABA statement of the song.

KEY CHANGE (MODULATION)

In the words of series editor Gregg Akkerman, "When musicians refer to the key of a song, they are referring to a pitch upon which the bulk of the music is centered around as its foundation or 'home base.' To accomplish variety or a shift in energy, [composer/arrangers sometimes] transition to a new key; this is called a key change [or modulation]." Modulation is part of the formal study of harmony and creates contrast and excitement to keep the music interesting or to move it from one emotional place to another. There are many ways to change key in an arrangement, and it is a fine art.

Key changes are noted when they occur. Sometimes they happen several times, as in Buddy Rich's recording of "Dateless Brown" (chapter 5). Most of the piece is in one sound center, and then at 1:24 we can hear a shift and finally land in a different sonic place at 1:34 when the trombone solos. At 2:11, the tonal center jumps to a new place and stays there until the drums solo at 2:49, and we are at yet another place, this time till the end.

THE EARLIEST DAYS

1800s–1919

Like any popular music trend or style, the big band era's roots are many and diverse. The concept of a dance orchestra led by a named leader dates to the 1800s. Back in the 1820s, violinist Joseph Lanner led his own dance orchestra in Austria; such was his popularity that he later formed four different orchestras under his own name to play ballrooms, beer gardens, concert rooms, and private mansions. One leader of a Lanner ensemble was none other than Johann Strauss, who soon formed his own ensemble and toured all over Europe. Strauss and his son were known for their original waltz compositions, which are still played and recorded.

In the 1840s, Nathaniel Gow led an orchestra that was the most popular ensemble in England. In the United States, an African American multi-instrumentalist born in Martinique named Francis Johnson became well-known among the elite on the East Coast for his dance ensembles as well as for his compositions. In 1837, he led the first American ensemble to tour in Europe and brought back Strauss waltzes to play in America. By the time of his death in 1844, he had toured as far west as St. Louis.

During the Civil War from 1861 to 1865, there were several military bands active on both sides of the conflict. After the war, many band instruments were discarded or given to young people who wanted to learn music, and demand for dance music reached an all-time high.

Music publishers prepared and sold arrangements of popular songs for both large and small orchestras; because they were sold by music dealers and were regularly stocked so that anyone could buy them, they came to be known as "stock" arrangements.

In the 1880s, Mexican bands were playing in New Orleans, so various streams of dance rhythms would eventually infuse the new music forming there. Ragtime's roots came from Spanish and Cuban dances such as the habanera, danza (derived from the European contradanza), tango (from Argentina), and maxixe; Ned Sublette has pointed out that Scott Joplin's popular rag "The Entertainer" has the rhythm of the Cuban danzón. By 1897, ragtime was just beginning to be played and heard all over the United States. Most rags were composed for piano and could only be played by skilled pianists, but since many homes from all strata of society had pianos, there was a ready market for something new. Stock arrangements of these new pieces could be purchased for band, orchestra, one or two guitars, banjos, and other solo instruments and combinations as well. Although there were many people—both white and black alike—who did not find this music "proper," it was the most up-to-date style of popular music until the mid-1910s. Renowned concert bandleader John Philip Sousa programmed arrangements of ragtime compositions in his concerts, although he himself did not care for the style.

By 1900, there were numerous black circus sideshow and tent show bands of between five and ten musicians that were heard across the country playing ragtime and syncopated music. The director of several excellent sideshow bands was P. G. Lowery, who was a mainstay for Ringling Bros. and Barnum & Bailey circus for years. Because of rampant racial prejudice during the post–Civil War era, these fine bands rarely played the main shows but certainly left their mark on listeners, playing the latest dance tunes, pop songs, and ragtime compositions. Another source for the new music being performed was touring minstrel shows; many listeners—black and white—heard blues songs for the first time at these presentations.

There were great opportunities for African American writers, composers, and performers beginning in the late 1890s. Elaborately staged shows written and directed by blacks but financed by white managers and investors toured all over the country except the South, and many of these shows even had successful Broadway runs. Called "big shows," such legendary names as Will Marion Cook, Bert Williams, George Walker, Bob Cole, and Ernest Hogan became stars. Central to the "big show" world by the early 1900s was composer, arranger, and conductor James Reese Europe, who became one of the most important arranger/ conductors in show business. He formed the Clef Club as a social organization, union, and booking office for black ensembles large and small. By 1913, Europe could call upon almost two hundred musicians for various-sized ensembles for all occasions. Europe was also a master of publicity, and in order to show off his musicians' versatility in performances of both concert and dance music, he organized several events all over New York City. A career highlight was a sold-out performance at Carnegie Hall in 1912, years before popular music became a programming staple in this illustrious concert space. In fact, many historians consider this the first jazz concert.

In 1913, Europe's Society Orchestra played a private party where Vernon and Irene Castle were attendees. The Castles were the most well-known dance team in the United States; they popularized social dancing among the wealthy and even set up their own dancing school called the Castle House. The Castles were so impressed by Europe's ensemble that Europe became their musical director and composed dance music for their appearances, often in collaboration with fellow bandleader Ford Dabney. It is said that Europe used some ideas from blues composer W. C. Handy and came up with the music for the foxtrot, still a very popular ballroom dance today. Sales of sheet music of dance pieces by Europe and other Clef Club members attested to the new interest in public dancing. In years past, dance halls were not places that "proper" ladies and gentlemen attended; in fact, many were simply places where men picked up prostitutes. Thanks to the Castles, public dancing became socially acceptable to the masses.

It was inevitable that a record company would want to capitalize on Europe's music and record it for dancing in private homes, and in 1913, the Victor Talking Machine Company signed an agreement with him to do just that. Historians are relatively sure that Europe was the first African American ensemble leader to make recordings for a major record label. The group was made up of banjos, mandolins, clarinet, cornet, drums, and percussion, although a full drum set could not be properly recorded at this time. These records sold so well that the Columbia Graphophone Company issued its own set of dance records with Dan Kildare's ensemble, released under the name "Joan Sawyer's Persian Garden Orchestra." Kildare was also a member of the Clef Club, and Sawyer was a popular exhibition dancer who owned her own club. All of these recordings highlight the popular dances of the time, and though they are not considered jazz and are outside the scope of this book, they document the kind of music the public was dancing to during those years.

Europe and the Castles were planning a tour of European countries with an ensemble of forty African American musicians, but World War I intervened, and Vernon Castle volunteered for the British Aviation Corps in 1915. By this time Europe had quit the Clef Club and set up the Tempo Club, and his ensembles continued to grow in popularity. Europe continued to promote the African American musician in other ways. He enlisted in the New York Infantry in 1916, passed an officer's examination, and was then asked to create a military band. The ensemble traveled all over France giving concerts before the men were called to fight alongside French troops; the group came to be known as the Hellfighters. By August 1918, the men were called back from the front to play in camps and hospitals all over France, and those who heard them got their first taste of the music of the future, which was being called jazz.

The word itself had been seen in newspapers in San Francisco as early as 1912 and was associated with both team sports and copulation; the music had been heard in rudimentary form as early as 1913 played by ensembles appearing in vaudeville, although in that same year, Art Hickman's dance orchestra was referred to as a jazz band in newspaper ads. When the New Orleans–based Tom Brown Orchestra played an engagement in Chicago in 1915, the musicians were surprised to hear their music referred to as jazz music; they considered the music they were playing an extension of ragtime. The word *jazz* was not used to describe such music in New Orleans, the so-called birthplace of jazz.

The first jazz record has long been accepted as recorded by the Original Dixieland Jazz Band (ODJB) from New Orleans. In 1917, they recorded "Livery Stable Blues" for the Victor Talking Machine Company, and this recording sold in large numbers. However, an increasing number of musicologists now believe a December 1916 recording of "Down Home Rag" on Emerson Records is the first jazz record, beating the ODJB by two months. Clarinetist Wilbur Sweatman, in the words of

Mark Berresford, "builds up the excitement via embellished phrases to an exciting final chorus where he wails and draws out the notes."

By 1919, there were many so-called jazz bands of three to five players elaborating and embellishing the melody; fully improvised solos would not be heard until the 1920s. Much of the music was crude and loud, often performed by instrumentalists who could not read music. On Hellfighters recordings recorded for Pathe in 1919, Europe's musicians certainly played freely and elaborated on what Europe wrote; listeners can hear why the French audiences who heard the band during the war went crazy for the new music. These recordings are an important introduction to what would become the big band music of the 1920s. Though they are performed by a smaller version of Europe's ensemble, they provide a fascinating glimpse of the new syncopated music played by a large group. In general, the recordings are not as stiff as the military bands of the period that we have on record, there are "breaks"—short passages played by soloists that may very well be improvised—and plenty of accompanying "noises" typical of early jazz ensembles. Pathe Freres promoted these as jazz recordings, probably to cash in on the hot new word in pop music.

Of the twenty-four recordings by the ensemble, two stand out as gems: "St. Louis Blues" and "Memphis Blues," both compositions by W. C. Handy.

What: "Memphis Blues" by W. C. Handy
Where: Pathe Studios, East 38th Street, New York
When: March 7[?], 1919

"Memphis Blues" was originally published in 1912, one of the earliest blues compositions to appear in sheet music form. Even though there are musical figures that are right out of ragtime, the rhythm is influenced by the Cuban dance, the habanera. The main theme of the melody played by the trumpets is accompanied by swooping trombones and reeds playing fills (0:06). The real thrill of the recording is when the music changes key and the verse is played, interspersed by written-out fills in the clarinets (1:25); buzzing trumpets can be heard not only playing the melodic statements but under a fill played by a solo trumpet (1:48). Two-bar breaks by trombone and clarinet interrupt the melody and the rhythm literally stops so that they are clearly the center of attention (2:02). A later fill is a trumpet playing "Reveille" (2:32).

What: "St. Louis Blues" by W. C. Handy
Where: Pathe Studios, East 38th Street, New York
When: March 3, 1919

"St. Louis Blues" was first recorded in 1916 by Columbia Records's house band led by Charles Adams Prince. It is rather formal and stiff sounding, with no instrumental contrast (trumpet plays the melody throughout); although it was meant for dancing, it is repetitious and becomes boring quickly. The Europe recording is in another class entirely! It starts out in the habanera rhythm with clarinets stating the melody. Brass come in next accompanied by castanets (0:06). Clarinets play the melody against muted trumpet growls (0:15), with trombones joining in on the repeat (0:32). The habanera returns for the next melodic statement (0:49), and then three held chords are heard (1:10). What is coming next? A solo cornet plays the melody against a soft background of glides, swoops, and growls by the ensemble (1:14). Two choruses by the clarinet are answered by cornet (1:50). The last two choruses are played by a clarinet solo, starting straight then embellishing the melody, with a countermelody by an oboe (2:24). The ensemble continues amid more growling and sliding (2:42), and then a short clarinet statement ends the setting.

One of the great developments in American ensemble music was the introduction of the saxophone. Developed by Belgian instrument maker Adolphe Sax in 1840, it was introduced into French military bands soon afterward. French composers began writing solo works and saxophone ensemble music by the 1850s.

But the saxophone never really caught on in the concert music world, and by 1900 it was thought of as strictly a band and novelty instrument. The most popular saxophone-playing group in the United States was the Six Brown Brothers, who made recordings, toured the vaudeville circuit, and appeared in Broadway shows. The saxophone was easy to learn, but like any instrument, real mastery took time and practice. Dance bands in San Francisco usually had one saxophone by

1915, and a saxophonist in the Frisco Jazz Band named Rudy Weidoeft astounded listeners with his virtuosic technique. By 1916, both alto and tenor saxophone parts were found in dance band stock arrangements, and saxophones were part of the pit orchestras of the famous Princess Theatre shows on Broadway, with songs by Jerome Kern. They were introduced by orchestrator Frank Saddler as a practicality; the Princess was a small theater with a small orchestra pit, and saxes doubled the strings and made the orchestra sound larger.

In 1913, the management of the St. Francis Hotel in San Francisco took the bold step of introducing public dancing by holding tea dances on Monday and Friday afternoons with a trio. These proved so successful that by 1914, two other hotels in the area began offering such events. In January 1915, Art Hickman led an ensemble that played supper dances from Monday through Friday at 9:00 pm and by 1919 had two saxophones in his band. By that time, the ODJB had spawned many small ensembles imitating their raucous sounds, so the sounds of jazz were in the public consciousness. Although larger ensembles avoided jazz directly, given that it was still thought of as vulgar and "too black" in some circles, any ensemble that had some aspects of the music was welcomed so that venues could say that they were offering the latest style. Hickman's ensemble received a great deal of notice as a result, and plans to record it date from as early as 1917. In 1919, the Columbia Graphophone Company signed a contract with Hickman, and the entire band traveled to New York in their own Pullman railroad car. The band played an engagement at the Biltmore Roof Hotel and made twenty-two released recordings over a two-week period. The band was an immediate hit with the hotel's affluent patrons, and producer Florenz Ziegfeld booked them for a week to play on the roof at the New Amsterdam Theatre, perhaps the most prestigious booking for a dance band in the entire country.

What: "The Hesitating Blues" by W. C. Handy
Where: Columbia Recording Studios, New York
When: September 20, 1919

Of all the recordings that the Hickman band made during this period, "The Hesitating Blues" comes the closest to small-group jazz of the era.

Both the soprano sax and clarinet wail through most of the recording, with everyone sounding like they are making the music up as they go along; one can imagine some listeners of the time thinking that these new sounds bordered on chaos. The rhythm is particularly loose sounding; drummer Hickman supports the band yet is playing quite freely. The record is also interesting in that another song is interpolated; after a statement of "The Hesitating Blues," the band plays a full chorus of "Beale Street Blues," another W. C. Handy composition (1:02). During "Beale Street Blues," the band plays the habanera rhythm (1:39) and returns to the jazz beat when "The Hesitating Blues" returns (2:21).

Hickman's recording shows that bands were incorporating the sounds of jazz as one style of their performances. The 1920s would continue this trend, but there would be many other ensembles—black and white—that would add their own ingredients into the dance music mix.

2

THE FIRST ERA

1920–1930

Socially, the decade of the 1920s brought many changes. Women finally had the vote and were entering the workforce, alcoholic beverages were illegal in the United States, fashion was less restrictive for both men and woman, and the nation as a whole was prosperous. The music of that era reflected these feelings of newness and progressiveness.

And by 1924, there were about nine hundred dance bands employing 7,200 musicians; the first era of the big band was flourishing. Four specific factors contributed to the popularity of the big bands in the 1920s: the continued construction of elaborate ballrooms, the popularity of radio, the improvement in sound recording, and the rise of the booking agency.

The construction of large ballrooms throughout the United States would satisfy the demands of young people wanting to socialize and dance the latest dances. Since the ballroom owners wanted to accommodate thousands of dancers per night, the only way to hear the music was if the band was made up of at least eight musicians. Many of these ballrooms became "taxi dance halls," where men of all ages purchased tickets and danced with girls for hire for two to three minutes per dance.

There were local big bands that played within a group of nearby cities, and other bands that performed within a certain group of states, which were called "territory bands," but there were several bands that were so popular that they toured not only across the United States but even in Europe.

By 1922, radio stations were being established all over the country; anybody with a modicum of talent could broadcast and even have his or her own show. Ensembles led by Paul Specht and Vincent Lopez were on the air as early as 1920 on experimental stations. By 1924, broadcasts emanated from radio studios, clubs, and ballrooms—WHN in New York featured Fletcher Henderson from the Club Alabam, Duke Ellington broadcast from the Kentucky Club, and pianist Earl Hines broadcast from KDKA in Pittsburgh. Listeners received the signals of radio stations hundreds of miles away (called DXing) and heard many regional bands after 11:00 pm. Networks—groups of stations sharing the same programming—were established late in the decade: NBC in 1926 and CBS in 1927, paving the way for large variety shows heard all over the country. Several name bands participated, spreading their fame even further. NBC had so many local stations that wanted to affiliate with the company that two NBC networks were created, known as the red and the blue.

Before 1925, most recordings were made by ensembles playing in front of a large horn, and the vibrations led to a cutter onto a wax blank; this was known as the acoustic or mechanical method. The sound was crude, similar to listening to music over an old telephone, and it took a long time to balance the different sound colors to get a good recording; musicians were placed all over the recording laboratory so that loud instruments stood in the back and softer instruments were right up against the horn. Strings in particular did not record well. But as early as 1920, microphones and amplification were used experimentally and became quite sophisticated so that by mid-1925, electric recording was adopted by most record companies, and recordings sounded vivid and more naturalistic. Finally the big bands could be heard far more accurately, and dynamics were more pronounced.

In the early 1920s, bands were usually booked by the leaders or a representative of the ensemble, and some leaders even created clones of their groups, performing under the leader's name even if the leader wasn't there. But Chicago bandleader and ophthalmologist Jules C. Stein realized that there was real money to be made in booking bands rather than leading them, so he formed Music Corporation of America (MCA) in 1924 with Billy Goodheart Jr. MCA went from booking engagements (or "gigs") in Chicago and the Midwest to managing bands, promising them more money, more gigs, and wide exposure. Then the company signed exclusives with dance halls; such palaces now had access to the best bands as long as they were MCA clients. In 1929, the Guy Lombardo Orchestra was the first name band on the MCA roster after Stein opened a New York office. He was soon offering deals to radio sponsors and even networks. But we've got some catching up to do before the management of bands became really big business. Some true pioneers were finding audiences and developing their ensembles.

As stated earlier, Chicago was an important city for music during the 1920s. Before World War I, the Windy City was the destination for large groups of African Americans from the South who aspired to a life of less racial prejudice and better paying jobs. After playing in vaudeville and touring, many musicians from New Orleans started playing dances on the South Side of Chicago. The legendary Joe "King" Oliver had a successful small band that played at Lincoln Gardens when he called for a musician who'd been his protégé in New Orleans. Louis Armstrong headed north to join his mentor, and the man called the first great jazz artist and improviser played second trumpet with Oliver every night. Musicians black and white came to listen and learn and bought their 1923 recordings on the Gennett and OKeh labels. Eventually Armstrong left to join Fletcher Henderson in New York, and later Oliver himself moved there to lead a large ensemble.

Some of the musicians who came to listen to Oliver and Armstrong were members of a dance orchestra led by tenor saxophonist and songwriter Isham Jones. By 1921 he had one of the top ensembles in Chicago, propelled by the success of his recordings on the Brunswick label and was already featuring "jazzy" novelties in his performances. Most of his arrangements were written by Harry L. Alford, a pioneer in forming and running a music arrangement service with an almost assembly-line proficiency for composers, performers, and publishers.

Jones had a star trumpet player named Louis Panico. Panico learned many of his performance "tricks" from King Oliver, who considered him a first-rate talent. Panico had a wide variety of novelty sounds and styles, such as laughing or simulating a baby crying (Panico even wrote a book for aspiring "novelty" cornetists). He himself did not think that he was a jazz soloist, but historians argue that he was a highly influential musician whose solos were jazz influenced, and such was his reputation that many musicians came to hear him, including Doc Cheatham and Bix Beiderbecke. Jones's recording of "Wabash Blues" reportedly sold two million copies and is a good example of how the Jones band played a jazz-inflected novelty as part of its repertoire in between ballads, foxtrots, and waltzes. It is not a strict twelve-bar blues but like many pieces of the time reflects the new looseness of the jazz style.

What: "Wabash Blues" by Dave Ringle and Fred Meinkin (based on "The Trombone Jazz" by Joseph E. Maddy); arranged by Harry L. Alford
Where: Brunswick Recording Laboratory, New York
When: August 1921

"Wabash Blues" starts out with a short introduction: a sliding trombone plays the melody while a soprano sax plays a sustained background and an alto sax plays a rhythmic background (0:10). The verse is heard played by Panico's lead (0:57). The trumpeter plays alone while the rhythm plays in stop time (i.e., the rhythm doesn't play on all the beats but only on some) (1:09). Saxes play a variation of the melody while the trumpet plays both straight and jazzy fills under them (1:21). Panico takes over the melody and plays in his "laughing" style until the end of the record (2:10).

In San Francisco in 1917, a violinist/violist named Paul Whiteman heard a small jazz band at a cafe. Whiteman was fascinated and soon put together his own seven-piece dance ensemble with jazzy elements. World War I intervened, and Whiteman enlisted in the navy and formed a jazz band there. Out of the service by 1918, he formed a new ensemble at the Fairmont Hotel, where he played afternoon tea dances and accompanied variety shows at night. By 1920, Whiteman's nine-piece band was booked at the prestigious Alexandria Hotel in Los Angeles; pianist Ferde Grofé was the chief arranger, notable since many orchestras were still adapting stock arrangements for their repertoire. When the band played at the prestigious Ambassador Hotel in Atlantic City, Victor Talking Machine executives signed the Whiteman band to a recording contract. Whiteman would remain at Victor for eight years,

and many of his records were top sellers. Whiteman's en.
the premiere band in the country during this initial era of t.

A concert of music at Aeolian Hall in New York on Fe.
1924, introduced George Gershwin's "Rhapsody in Blue" and ce.
Whiteman's success even further. He even started his own bo.
agency, sending out Whiteman Orchestras all over the country; at one
time, there were sixty-eight of them, all sharing the same arrangements
as the original ensemble. For a price, Whiteman even showed up for a
few minutes if he was in the neighborhood.

Even though his publicists insisted that he was the "king of jazz,"
Whiteman's ensemble was a dance band that featured a few jazz
players. In 1926, he wanted more jazz soloists in his band, and for a
time he had Tommy and Jimmy Dorsey and Red Nichols. He admired
the musicians in the Jean Goldkette Orchestra (which is discussed later), and when Goldkette disbanded in 1927, he hired some of his best
soloists, such as the legendary C-melody saxophonist Frank Trumbauer
and cornetist Bix Beiderbecke; he also hired Goldkette chief arranger
Bill Challis to bring the Goldkette sound to the Whiteman band, and
Challis re-created the Goldkette book for Paul. Even die-hard jazz enthusiasts were now paying attention to Whiteman's ensemble.

What: "Changes" by Walter Donaldson; arranged by Bill Challis
Where: Victor Talking Machine Recording Laboratory, Chicago
When: November 23, 1927

This is the first recording of Bix Beiderbecke with the Whiteman Orchestra. By this time, Beiderbecke had established himself as one of the
most important cornet soloists in music, and historians have noted that
although Louis Armstrong's playing was "hot" and powerful, Beiderbecke's was often more laid-back and "cooler." The two artists had great
admiration for each other, Armstrong calling him "my boy Bix" in his
writings.

By this time, Whiteman had nineteen musicians, a trio of crooning
male singers called the "Sweet Trio," and a trio of "hot" singers called
the "Rhythm Boys," of which Bing Crosby was a member. All of them
appear on this recording.

After a brief introduction, Challis uses three harmonized baritone saxophones, trumpets, and strings to play alternate phrases of the melody (0:10). A short transition leads to the verse played by the full ensemble (0:52); the vocal is sung by Whiteman's "Sweet Trio" (1:11) then taken over by the "Rhythm Boys," with Bing Crosby featured (1:47), then Bix Beiderbecke takes a solo that is now considered a classic (2:05) and alerted listeners that the Whiteman Orchestra could play a true "hot" sound after years of flirting with the style. The full band takes over (2:23) and ends the recording after a short statement by alto saxophonist Chester Hazlett (2:40).

Fortunately, another take exists of "Changes" with an entirely different Beiderbecke solo. It is listed in the Recorded Resources chapter under the link for the first take.

Here is another excellent Beiderbecke solo that cannot be left out of any book on jazz and big band.

What: "Lonely Melody" by Sam Coslow, Benny Meroff, and Hal Dyson; arranged by Bill Challis
Where: Liederkrantz Hall, 111 East 58th Street, New York
When: January 4, 1928

After a quote from an Irving Berlin song, "A Pretty Girl is Like a Melody," the melody is played by the full band (0:11). After a transition (0:57), the verse is played by the ensemble (1:02), which leads to Bix's solo (1:23), the B part of the song played straight by Charles Strickfadden on tenor sax (1:44). Beiderbecke returns, and then the song is heard in a hot jazz trio (Frank Trumbauer on C-melody sax, Jimmy Dorsey on alto, and Chester Hazlett on tenor) (2:04), violins play the bridge (2:26), and then the full band is heard until a clarinet solo by Jimmy Dorsey ends the recording (2:47).

Once again, most fortunately, there's an alternate take available of this arrangement, and the solo by Bix is totally different. This performance may be found on Spotify; look under *The Indispensable Bix Beiderbecke*.

Although some jazz fans of the period thought that being with Whiteman held Bix back, Beiderbecke was proud to be part of the most popular band in the country and enjoyed his stay until he was ultimately forced to quit for health reasons. The sides Whiteman made with Bix are highly prized examples of big band jazz in the late 1920s and certainly exposed much of the general public to the new music.

Fletcher Henderson was a chemistry student at Columbia University who took a job with one of the first African American–owned record labels in 1921, Black Swan. He began putting together ensembles for dance gigs, and his band became one of the house bands at Roseland, one of the most prestigious ballrooms in the country. Although the orchestra played its share of Foxtrots, tangos, and waltzes, the ensemble also played and recorded blues pieces with improvised solos. In 1924, Henderson hired Louis Armstrong to join the band, and an important chapter in American music began. Armstrong immediately fired the band up with his powerful personality and drive, and recordings of the period show that his bluesy musical style permeated the entire band's sound.

What: "Copenhagen," by Walter Melrose and Charles Davis (adapted from the stock arrangement by Don Redman)
Where: Vocalion Studios, New York
When: October 30, 1924

"Copenhagen" is now considered a jazz classic and is still played by traditional Dixieland groups. Many recordings of the tune were made in 1924, and this is thought to be the best of all of them. It begins with an opening reed statement going up and down the scale, then an eight-bar blues melody (0:18) and various different statements that are repeated. Armstrong has a short solo (0:44). Full ensemble is heard (0:58), and then brass play figures answered by reeds (1:14). Charlie Green's trombone calls (1:49), the band responds (1:54), and this is repeated. A Buster Bailey clarinet solo in the low register is heard against a soft background (2:16). Throughout the rhythm drops out during melodic statements; this was not done very often, but dancers rarely had a problem regardless.

Henderson's was one of several bands who made records for several labels. Here's an example of two different performances of the same song, with two separate arrangements.

**What: "Shanghai Shuffle" by Gene Rodemich and Larry
Conley; arranged by Don Redman (adapted from the C. E.
Wheeler stock arrangement)
Where: Pathe Studios, East 38th Street, New York
When: ca. October 13, 1924**

Kaiser Marshall's cymbal and tom-tom drum give this an ethnic flavor,
something desirable during an era of new sounds and rhythms. Melody
is played by trumpets with wa-wa trombone (0:12), and saxes take over
with brass fills (0:30). Trombonist Charlie Green plays a muted trombone solo (1:05). Don Redman plays the melody on oboe, an instrument not commonly found in dance bands of the period (1:39). Armstrong plays a very strong solo using a mute open and closed for a wa-wa
effect (1:55). The last part of the record features the entire band (2:30),
the introduction is repeated (3:04), and the drum has the last word.

**What: "Shanghai Shuffle" by Gene Rodemich and Larry
Conley; arranged by Don Redman (adapted from the C. E.
Wheeler stock arrangement)
Where: Vocalion Studios, New York
When: November 7, 1924**

This is almost an entirely different arrangement. Perhaps the Vocalion
label wanted something a bit more straightforward than the jazzier
treatment on Pathe. The biggest differences are that this recording
relies less on the drums, and Armstrong's and Green's solos are on open
horn rather than muted.

Saxes play the melody (0:21), and then the melody is played by brass
(0:54). Louis Armstrong plays a spectacular solo on open horn (1:10).
Saxes play the melody high in their register (1:43), and then there is a
solo by trombonist Charlie Green (2:00). Perhaps it is Green who yells
"Whoopee hey hey" (2:16). Just like the Pathe recording, the full band
plays a variant of the melody (notice the Charleston rhythm at 2:18)
until the end.

Henderson attracted many of the best black musicians for the remainder of the decade, and when Don Redman left to lead McKinney's Cotton Pickers, Henderson took over as chief arranger himself. But he still had outside arrangers such as John Nesbitt and Benny Carter.

What: "Blazin'" by Joe Sanders; arranged by Benny Carter
Where: Columbia Phonograph Studios, New York
When: June 16, 1929

This is an excellent example of how hot this band had become by the late 1920s. Gone were many of the musicians who were part of the original band. Rex Stewart and Bobby Stark were now playing cornet and trumpet respectively, Clarence Holiday (Billie Holiday's father) was playing banjo, John Kirby was playing string bass and tuba, and Walter Johnson was the drummer.

"Blazin'" is a showcase for the band's soloists. Tenor saxophonist Coleman Hawkins plays a solo interspersed with band statements (0:04). Stark has a solo (0:28) before the band takes off roaring (0:41). Another example of "call and response" is heard between the saxophones and the brass (1:00). Trombonist Jimmy Harrison solos (1:09), and the band takes off again (1:18). Rex Stewart exchanges solos with alto saxophonist Harvey Boone (called "trading") after a key change (1:36). Hawkins trades with first Stark and Stewart (1:53), Henderson gets a small solo (2:13), then full band until a short statement by Boone and then Stewart again to end the side.

Henderson's band recorded prolifically under its own name and as the Dixie Stompers. Unfortunately, Henderson was never a good manager and was not affiliated with a booking agency when such agencies began taking over the band business. His story continues throughout this book.

Some bandleaders appear in several chapters of this book. Duke Ellington is our first subject who led bands for many years even after the big band era unofficially ended. He got his start in Washington, D.C., as a pianist/bandleader and went to New York City to play with Wilbur Sweatman but returned to Washington after only a few months due to lack of work. Returning in 1923 with other musicians who would be with him for years, they played in a band called the Washingtonians. By 1924, Ellington had become the leader of the ensemble. In 1926, agent/ publisher Irving Mills signed a contract with Ellington, giving himself 45 percent of everything Ellington earned. In addition to promoting the band and booking gigs, Mills published Ellington's compositions and made agreements with record companies so Duke's band could record. In December 1927, Ellington's band was the house orchestra at the Cotton Club, an exclusive nightclub featuring revues with songs written by the top composers of the day, interspersed with dance numbers written by Ellington in what was described as "jungle style" music. Between 1927 and 1930, the band broadcast more than two hundred programs a year during the afternoon and late in the evening, exposing more and more listeners to Ellington's unique compositions and soloists.

From the very beginning, Ellington collected excellent musicians to add to his ensemble, and his band would always be considered an all-star band. During this period, he had alto/soprano saxophonist Johnny Hodges, trumpeter Bubber Miley, trombonist Joe "Tricky Sam" Nanton, clarinetist Barney Bigard, and baritone saxophonist Harry Carney—all of whom are now considered important improvisational voices in jazz history. These disparate artists combined to create a unique sound that has never been matched by any other band. Duke often said that he wrote music based on both his musicians' strengths and weaknesses, often writing entire pieces to feature them.

Ellington recorded some of his pieces several times for several different record companies under such names as the Harlem Footwarmers, the Jungle Band, and the Whoopee Makers. These records were unique in that in many circles, Ellington's music was treated as not only dance, but concert music; European listeners considered him an important composer in a new American-made medium, elevating Ellington's importance and the jazz/dance ensemble at the same time.

Ellington was a master at using a short riff (melodic idea) to form the basis of a song or formal composition. Often these riffs came from the musicians in his orchestra while they were noodling around on their instruments. Duke was also a master of changing and restructuring compositions and arrangements; when a new musician joined the band, that artist quickly found that the parts in his book were worthless, as there'd been so much music that had been changed or rearranged.

"The Mooche" was played frequently for about two years, put aside, and then put back in the book by the late 1940s for the remainder of the band's existence. Ellington was not one to look backward, but like many of his songs and compositions, "The Mooche" was popular enough that different treatments of it were featured through the years.

What: "The Mooche" by Duke Ellington
Where: OKeh Recording Laboratory, New York
When: October 1, 1928

Comparing two contemporary recordings of "The Mooche" is enlightening and instructive: enlightening to hear how utterly singular this orchestra was because of the different personalities that Ellington featured and instructive to see how he refined a piece until he was satisfied.

The recording opens with clarinets playing the harmonized melody in their high register, moving downward, snakelike, interrupted by plunger-muted bursts by trumpeter James "Bubber" Miley. The second phrase of the melody (0:08) moves even further downward, once again followed by more Miley. There is an eight-bar extension with clarinets playing held notes as Miley continues to intersperse musical comments (0:31), and the piece shifts from minor to major, as brass play a new melody (0:46). The composition returns to minor as Barney Bigard plays a written solo in the lower register of his clarinet, with comments by a guest, legendary twelve-string blues guitarist Lonnie Johnson (1:09). Johnson continues as a scat vocal solo in major by Baby Cox (Gertrude Davis) follows for twelve bars, one of three recordings by this popular black Broadway personality (1:32). Miley then solos in minor with Hodges commenting (1:55). The record ends as it started, with the snake-like melody in clarinets with Miley comments (2:19), and the eight-bar transition is heard with Miley having the last word.

A second recording of "The Mooche" followed a few days later.

What: "The Mooche" by Duke Ellington
Where: Brunswick Recording Laboratory #2, New York
When: October 17, 1928

This recording begins with a new, sustained eight-bar introduction that becomes louder and then softer, setting a sinister mood. The recording proceeds in the same way as on the October 1 date, but changes as the new melody is now a solo by pianist Ellington (0:57), which then proceeds to the Bigard solo with no commentary (1:19), moves on to the Miley solo with Hodges (1:43), and then Hodges has his own twelve-bar solo in major (2:07). The ending of the record includes the new sinister introduction, the clarinet melody, and the transition. Miley plays fills under the melody and transition (2:30).

Both of these performances are wonderful, but the second performance has more compositional contrast (the solo in major by Hodges after Miley's makes the piece more balanced). "The Mooche" shows us why Ellington the composer is so highly regarded—this is clearly not just a melody with some riffs, fills, improvised solos, and then a melodic restatement to end the recording. This is a thought-out, planned composition incorporating the elements of dance music and jazz. It is also an early example of how Ellington would use the blues form in many different guises and styles.

Ellington recorded several pieces that he wrote for Cotton Club shows. "Cotton Club Stomp" was later featured in a twenty-minute film titled "Black and Tan Fantasy."

What: "Cotton Club Stomp" by Duke Ellington
Where: Liederkranz Hall, 111 East 58th Street, New York
When: May 3, 1929

After a dramatic introduction, the band settles into a hot groove with baritone saxophonist Harry Carney soloing over the full ensemble (0:08). Trumpeter Freddie Jenkins solos over the rhythm section (0:42). Alto saxophonist Johnny Hodges has the next solo with rhythm accompaniment (1:13), followed by a solo from clarinetist Barney Bigard (1:45). (An observation: the band is so good here that the original recording director let flubbed notes by Jenkins and a squeak by Bigard pass, very unusual during any era of recording.) The full band returns (2:19) with Bigard and Carney adding some comments.

Jean Goldkette was a concert pianist who was born in either France or Greece but came to the United States and settled in Detroit, where he led and booked bands; he also co-owned the popular Greystone Ballroom. From 1924 to 1927, he led an ensemble that included musicians such as Bix Beiderbecke (cornet), Frank Trumbauer (C-melody saxophone), Steve Brown (bass), Bill Rank (trombone), Eddie Lang (guitar), Tommy Dorsey (trombone and trumpet), and Jimmy Dorsey (clarinet, saxophone). Arranging the music was Bill Challis. At its height, the Goldkette band played opposite Fletcher Henderson's ensemble at Roseland and won the "battle." Henderson trumpet soloist Rex Stewart later wrote that Goldkette's was "the original predecessor to any large white dance orchestra that followed, up to Benny Goodman."

At that time, some record labels segregated the ensembles that recorded for them, with black bands playing their hotter arrangements but not recording their other dance repertoire, and white ensembles playing commercial music but not their jazzier pieces. As a result, Goldkette wasn't able to record much of his "hot" repertoire. But the few titles that the band did do show why its hot repertoire is now considered legendary.

What: "My Pretty Girl" by Charles Fulcher; arranged by Bill Challis
Where: Liederkranz Hall, 111 East 58th Street, New York
When: February 1, 1927

After a short introduction, the ensemble sounds as if it is making the music up as it goes along, with improvising instruments surrounding the harmonized ensemble (0:08). We then come to a melodic line played by the trombone (Spiegel Wilcox playing into a megaphone) and a Danny Polo clarinet solo (0:29), a short break by Trumbauer (0:57), then full ensemble. When listening to this section, pay particular attention to the bass playing of Steve Brown. He is playing rather freely, keeping the beat going but playing like a soloist, even slapping the strings and making them snap. This whole section sounds loose and free, and yet the rhythm is steady, quite a feat. A short break by Bill Rank follows (1:26), and then Joe Venuti plays a violin solo (1:28) alternating with the full ensemble. The last chorus features the band and more Steve Brown bass, a solo by Trumbauer (2:05), and then full ensemble until the end.

What: "Clementine (from New Orleans)" by Henry Creamer and Harry Warren; arranged by Bill Challis
Where: Liederkranz Hall, 111 East 58th Street, New York
When: September 15, 1927

The band plays the melody after a short introduction (0.10), Bill Rank plays the melody for the bridge (B) (0.31), then full band again (0.42). The verse is played with fills by the legendary guitarist Eddie Lang (0.55), and the sax section plays a variant of the melody (I refer to such written-out variations of the melody for an instrumental section as a paraphrase) (1.14). Bix solos (1.58), interrupted by Joe Venuti's hot violin in the bridge (2.20), followed by a band finish.

I must comment on the sound quality of these and several other recordings made at Liederkranz Hall. This legendary room was built in 1881 as part of the Liederkranz club, a German American choral society. Its acoustics were so impressive that the Victor Talking Machine Company turned it into one of the finest recording studios ever constructed; it was later used by Columbia Records. In 1950, the hall became a television studio, a sad loss to the recording world. We revisit this studio again in the pages to come.

Goldkette was forced to disband in 1927 due to the high expense of the band members' salaries. As stated above, many were hired by Paul Whiteman and changed that ensemble for the better.

Drummer Ben Pollack first attracted some attention in the jazz world playing with the New Orleans Rhythm Kings. In 1925, he formed an orchestra in California but returned to his hometown of Chicago in 1926. This first ensemble featured a young Benny Goodman on clarinet and Glenn Miller playing trombone. Cornet player Jimmy McPartland joined in 1927, and trombone legend Jack Teagarden was added in 1928. Reed player Joseph "Fud" Livingston and Miller were the arrangers. In that same year, the Pollack band began a long-term prestigious engagement at the Park Central Hotel in New York City and began recording for the Victor Talking Machine Company.

Pollack faced the same challenges as Goldkette in that Victor chose what repertoire his band could record, but since the new jazz style with improvised solos was popular with the college crowd, a few gems were preserved.

What: "Singapore Sorrows" by Jack LeSoir and Ray Doll; arranged by Joseph "Fud" Livingston
Where: Liederkranz Hall, 111 East 58th Street, New York
When: April 6 and April 28, 1928

Note: Happily, there are four different performances (takes) of this title. The timings reflect the original issue, which is take six.

"Singapore Sorrows" is a classic example of the chinoiserie craze in the United States and Europe at the time, when Chinese food, art, and culture were new and fascinated the public (another Chinese-themed song that was written in the 1920s that is still quite popular is "Limehouse Blues"). This is also a great example of a performance that was meant to appeal to the general public, offering some jazz seasoning in the rendition. The recording starts off with an introduction begun by temple blocks leading to full ensemble (with a gong included). The melody switches between baritone sax and trumpet-led ensemble for a chorus (0.10), the verse is played by clarinets in the high register (0.50), then the song is sung by Ben Pollack (1.09). Now the track comes alive with a Benny Goodman solo (1.47), and this recording proves that at the age of nineteen, he was already an excellent improviser. A trombone solo by Glenn Miller follows (2.05), which should surprise those who know him only as an arranger/bandleader. A band transition (2.22) leads to a powerful Jimmy McPartland cornet solo (2.31), and the recording ends after another statement by the entire band.

Pollack continued leading excellent bands throughout the thirties and discovered other musicians who would become legendary; Harry James played in his band before James joined Benny Goodman. But Pollack was all but forgotten in later years, and in 1971, he committed suicide.

Born in Panama, Luis Russell had been in several bands in New Orleans when he moved to Chicago to play with King Oliver. Oliver moved to New York and Russell went with him, eventually taking over most of Oliver's sidemen and adding a few others to create a big band. The ensemble was one of the most exciting of the era thanks to the rhythm section of Danny Barker (guitar), Pops Foster (bass), and Paul Barbarin (drums), all New Orleans music veterans, creating a beat that was infectious and got audiences on the dance floor. The band also boasted excellent soloists such as J. C. Higgenbotham (trombone), and Henry "Red" Allen (trumpet). Russell's ensemble replaced Fletcher Henderson's band at Roseland for a time, a true mark of its quality. Band members would later say that Russell's band was like a family; everyone cheering everyone else on. Louis Armstrong was such a fan that he took over the band in 1935.

In 1929, Russell made some spectacular recordings, one of which is "Jersey Lightning."

What: "Jersey Lightning" by Luis Russell
Where: OKeh Recording Laboratories, New York
When: September 6, 1929

The first thing to notice is how fast the tempo is and how precisely the band plays the scale-like melody at such a blistering tempo, interrupted by clarinet bursts by Albert Nicholas with no rhythm under him. A piano solo by Russell (0:28) is backed by guitar, bass, and drums; note the exciting cymbal work by Barbarin. A brass statement follows (0:41), and then the melody returns, but with Foster playing exciting breaks (0:54). His sound is huge and his technique solid. A change of key leads to Red Allen's blustering solo (1:22). A sax section soli chorus takes over to keep the momentum going (1:49); notice how tight this section is as they play this devilishly difficult passage. J. C. Higgenbotham on trombone and Charlie Holmes on alto sax trade solos (2:15), and the band plays an out chorus (the final part of an arrangement that takes the band out) with Allen and Holmes commenting (2:43). The band slows down for the ending, bringing this performance to a close.

This recording certainly proves that the Russell band was one of the great ensembles of its time, even though it is not discussed as often as other bands of the period. Based on the sheer virtuosity of the ensemble playing, excellent solos, plus the excitement of the rhythm section, historians believe that this ensemble was one of the first true swing bands.

In 1926, drummer William McKinney put together a dance band in Detroit that he called McKinney's Cotton Pickers, an unfortunately racist name. In 1927, Fletcher Henderson's arranger Don Redman was invited to become the band's musical director, and the band became a popular national attraction. Several McKinney recordings had guest musicians, and the record chosen here features another star in the Fletcher Henderson Orchestra who popularized the tenor sax, the legendary stylist Coleman Hawkins.

What: "Wherever There's a Will, Baby" by Don Redman
Where: Liederkranz Hall, 111 East 58th Street, New York
When: November 7, 1929

After a brassy introduction, the melody is played by harmonized saxes with brass fills in between (another example of call and response) (0:08). The trumpeter Sidney DeParis plays the verse (0:42), and then we hear a Don Redman "vocal" where Redman recites the lyrics of the song accompanied by the rhythm section (0:59). After a brass fanfare (1:30), Hawkins takes over with his big, booting sound and excellent technique (1:34). For the out chorus, saxes and brass go back and forth with musical statements (more call and response) (2:11), an exciting piano solo by another guest, the legendary pianist/composer "Fats" Waller (2:20), full band, and then as the recording ends, there's a short alto sax solo by Benny Carter.

Redman left in 1931 to assemble his own band, which is discussed in the next chapter.

In Europe, some American hot band recordings were available, but the audiences for such recordings were relatively small. This didn't stop some British bandleaders from playing hot music, and two leaders in particular put together ensembles that featured jazz, with some help from American instrumentalists.

Bert Ambrose was a violinist who led ensembles both in the United States and England. An engagement at the Embassy Club in London led to an important residency at the Mayfair Hotel, where the ensemble played for dances and broadcasts for six years. The patronage at the Mayfair was primarily upper class and included the Prince of Wales. Guitarist and banjoist Joe Brannelly was an American who'd played with Ambrose in the United States, and two other American musicians were featured: Sylvester Ahola (trumpet) and Danny Polo (clarinet), who played with Bix Beiderbecke and Frank Trumbauer.

What: "Do Something" by Bud Green and Sam Stept; arranged by Lew Stone
Where: Chenil Galleries, Chelsea, London
When: June 2, 1929

When Jimmy Dorsey heard the 1929 Ambrose ensemble, he declared it the best dance band he'd ever heard. Unfortunately, their recordings during this period were recorded in a makeshift studio and sound dry and distorted; these are among the earliest recorded by the Decca Record Company, later to become Universal Music.

The introduction is out of tempo, unusual in a dance record in which one would expect the very beginning to be in tempo. A hot cymbal solo brings in the ensemble in tempo with trumpet lead by Sylvester Ahola (0:21). Future bandleader Ted Heath solos on trombone (0:43) with violin background, then back to ensemble. A break by baritone saxophonist Joe Crossman leads to saxes playing an improvised-sounding section with baritone sax lead (1:01), followed by a trumpet solo by Ahola (who years later would speak of his solo with pride) (1:28). Next comes a violin solo by Eric Siday (1:48) (who would later come to the United States and write electronic music), followed by more saxophone ensemble (1:58). The full ensemble takes over (2:11), followed by a Danny Polo clarinet solo (2:34). Brass return with clarinets playing an improvised-sounding harmonized line with baritone sax fills (2:46). The ending is a series of contrasts: a statement by clarinets (2:54), one by trumpets (2:56), and another by tenor sax, baritone sax, and trombone (2:59). Hot cymbal work and the orchestra with a violin melody line end this recording.

The rhythm section in this band is rock steady and strong without being overpowering, perfect for Ambrose's dancing public at the Mayfair Hotel. Reviews in such trade publications as *Melody Maker* rhapsodized over Ambrose's recordings, although they were poorly distributed and didn't sell well. Bert Ambrose continued to front excellent ensembles into the 1950s but later said that of all the bands he led, the ensemble from the late 1920s was his favorite.

Fred Elizalde was a concert pianist born in Spain who studied in London and then went to the United States to study composition. He led a big band at the Cinderella Roof in Los Angeles while he pursued his music studies and decided to form a "hot" dance band when he returned to London. He had a residency at the posh Savoy Hotel, and several outstanding American musicians joined the orchestra as players and arrangers, such as Joseph "Fud" Livingston, Adrian Rollini, and Chelsea Quealey. But older patrons did not like his music, and in 1929, his contract was not renewed. In 1931, he left jazz to pursue a concert music career and wrote numerous compositions played throughout Europe.

When Livingston joined the band, he brought some of his arrangements for Ben Pollack with him, and we get an opportunity to hear the same arrangement of "Singapore Sorrows" played by the Elizalde band.

What: "Singapore Sorrows" by Jack LeSoir and Ray Doll; arranged by Joseph "Fud" Livingston
Where: Parlophone Studios, London
When: April 12, 1929

The main differences between this recording and Pollack's are (1) the band is larger, and it even includes a harp, although it is almost inaudible, (2) there are no temple blocks, (3) the melody at the beginning is played by Adrian Rollini's bass saxophone (0:11), (4) the vocal is replaced by the melody played by three violins alternating with woodwinds (1:11), (5) the soloists are Bobby Davis (clarinet) (1:50), Frank Coughlan (trombone) (2:07), and Chelsea Quealey (trumpet) (2:33). The soloists are indeed better on Pollack's recording, but this treatment is slightly faster and more exciting in general.

A large segment of the American and European public was clearly jazz mad during the 1920s. But as we saw from examination of the Elizalde ensemble, an all-jazz band was certain to fail (Louis Armstrong's visit to England in 1932 was greeted by rabid fans and bemused listeners, the bemused outnumbering the rabid). And bad times were coming: the American stock market crash would have a devastating impact on many aspects of life, particularly the live and recorded music world. As we will see, the growth of radio and elaborate programs offering free entertainment caused many bands to break up, but there were some bright spots on the horizon.

3

INTERLUDE

1930–1935

The Depression changed many things in American life. The college crowd that went to ballrooms to hear their favorite bands during the 1920s now had families that they needed to support in a terrible economy, which didn't allow much, if any, money to go out dancing, and many ensembles were forced to disband due to lack of gigs. Radio was now the entertainment of choice for most Americans—it was free! Dance bands were represented, though. In 1931, CBS and both NBC networks aired fourteen dance shows weekly. By 1934, there were two dozen, many during prime time, and there were more shows aired on local stations, as many had staff orchestras of their own. But the music was often bland and there was little jazz content to be found. The white musicians who played in the popular bands of the 1920s were now staff musicians with the radio networks and earned excellent salaries playing for any number and types of programs. Such musicians as Artie Shaw commented years later that he did this work only for the money, for the music itself was terrible.

The record business was also in horrible shape. In 1929, seventy million records sold; by 1933, that number dwindled to four million, and some companies almost went bankrupt while others went out of business altogether.

But some ensembles continued playing the dates that remained, and there were several classic recordings by big bands during this era that had excellent jazz.

Bennie Moten was a pianist whose home base was Kansas City. His earliest recordings date from 1923 and reflect the New Orleans style as played by Louis Armstrong and King Oliver, but by 1926, the orchestra had absorbed the sophisticated sounds of such orchestras as Fletcher Henderson and Jean Goldkette. In 1929, Moten hired William "Count" Basie to play piano and Oran "Hot Lips" Page to play trumpet. Bandleader Walter Page joined when his own orchestra disbanded, and a new, relaxed, easy swing can be heard on the band's records that was the beginning of the so-called Kansas City sound.

The Moten Orchestra made several great recordings for OKeh and Victor, but perhaps their finest sides were their last. Reportedly, the ensemble arrived at Victor's Camden, New Jersey, recording studios broke and starving. After feasting on stew, they proceeded to record ten sides that are now considered classics.

What: "Moten Swing," credited to Bennie and Buster Moten, but most likely written by Count Basie and Eddie Durham; arranged by Durham
Where: Victor Church Studios, 114 North Fifth Street, Camden, New Jersey
When: December 13, 1932

The harmonic structure of "Moten Swing" is exactly the same as the popular song "You're Driving Me Crazy" from 1930, an early example of a piece using the same chord pattern as a pop song (we see a lot of this in jazz from the 1940s onward). The record opens with the great Count Basie playing a piano solo backed by Walter Page's bass and Willie McWashington's drums. The sound quality on this recording is so good that you'll notice that the bass is playing on every beat, a major change in rhythmic feeling from bands of the 1920s, where the bass plays on beats one and three. Saxes and brass then trade rhythmic figures for the middle part of the tune (0:19), and then Basie continues his solo. The first chorus by the saxes and brass alludes to the melody without stating it as Basie continues to fill in on piano (0:38). Eddie Durham puts down his trombone to take a solo on guitar (0:57), and then saxes finish out the chorus (1:07). Saxophonist Eddie Barefield solos as brass fill (1:17), and then after a key change, trumpet player Hot Lips Page solos as saxes play under him (1:57), with a short solo by tenor saxophonist Ben Webster in the middle of Page's chorus (2:16). At this point we finally hear the melody fully stated by the whole band during the last chorus (2:36).

Moten continued taking whatever gigs came his way and was about to audition for a job at the prestigious Grand Terrace Ballroom when he entered the hospital for a tonsillectomy and the doctor accidentally severed his jugular vein, and he died. Basie put together a new nine-piece band named Barons of Rhythm, which included former Moten musicians. That ensemble would make musical history.

British bassist, composer, and bandleader Patrick "Spike" Hughes was a classically trained musician who loved jazz and made several excellent recordings for the U.K. Decca label. He came to the United States and put together an all-star orchestra with the help of John Hammond and arranger, saxophonist, and trumpeter Benny Carter. All of the records are excellent, but several are masterpieces. They were released in England as Spike Hughes and His Negro Orchestra.

What: "Firebird" by Spike Hughes
Where: Brunswick Recording Studios, 1776 Broadway, New York
When: May 19, 1933

Hughes became a real student of the music. Like many Europeans, he listened carefully to the new sounds and compositions of the Duke Ellington Orchestra, but he also loved the Fletcher Henderson and Benny Carter orchestras. "Firebird" provides a nice mix of all of these orchestral styles, and it showcases some of the great soloists of the period.

After a short introduction with saxes trilling (a musical device that occurs throughout the recording), saxes play the first part of the melody in harmony with brass punctuations (0:09). Notice that the lead saxophone is a soprano, played by Carter. Brass take over the middle part of the melody with sax trills (0:26), then saxes return to finish the melody. Solos begin with two giants of the tenor saxophone trading a solo chorus, Leon "Chu" Berry (0:51) and Coleman Hawkins (1:07). Luis Russell alumnus Henry "Red" Allen takes a full chorus with sax background (1:24) and shows that although he absorbed the Louis Armstrong style, he is his own man harmonically, playing some notes that don't belong to the harmony but making them work. Trombonist William "Dicky" Wells solos on trombone (1:57). The key changes (2:30), and the brass play rhythmic figures against the saxes (2:32). Then something truly unusual happens: Wayman Carver plays an improvised solo on the flute (2:49), an instrument rarely heard in a big band at that time (he would later play with the Chick Webb Orchestra). The entire band finishes up (2:57), brass punching out the melody with sax fills, which include trilling sections at the end.

These records created quite a stir in England, as this seems to be the only time that a white British composer directed a black group before World War II. Ironically, the recordings were not issued in the United States until the 1950s. Hughes realized that for him, these recordings would never be bettered, so he left jazz behind, taking a position as music critic at the *Daily Herald*. He also wrote program notes when Duke Ellington appeared in England in 1933.

Don Redman left McKinney's Cotton Pickers, returned to New York, and organized his own orchestra. His theme became one of the most distinctive compositions of that early period.

What: "Chant of the Weed" by Don Redman
Where: Brunswick Recording Studios, 799 Seventh Avenue, New York
When: September 24, 1931

Redman's ensemble was yet another group of all-star musicians: trumpeters Bill Coleman and Henry "Red" Allen, trombonists Claude Jones and Benny Morton, and pianist Horace Henderson. For his first recording date, Redman wrote this ode to marijuana use (there were others during that period: Cab Calloway can be seen in a movie singing "Reefer Man"). Harmonically adventurous, this composition became a classic almost immediately; even Duke Ellington had an arrangement of it in the 1960s, written by none other than Don Redman.

Written in AABA song form, cup-muted harmonized brass play against a saxophone unison during the first part of the A section, answered by harmonized saxes. Notice the drummer is playing temple blocks (0:06). The B section is saxes interspersed by brass (0:29). The A section returns and then there is a transition to the verse (0:55). Redman solos on alto saxophone, and he is the main focus except for a brief statement by trombones (1:20). Saxophones transition to a piano solo (2:22). Saxes have a paraphrase of the melody as brass fill (2:36). The beginning of the piece returns (2:50) to end the recording.

Redman kept the orchestra together for several years until he disbanded and freelanced. He later became Pearl Bailey's musical director and passed away in 1964.

Thanks to Irving Mills's management, Duke Ellington's Orchestra toured and appeared in movies. The band made its first tour of England and Scotland in 1933 and then toured Europe in 1934. European composers of concert music lauded him, his ensemble, and his compositions, and though Ellington was truly moved, that was balanced by the racism his band experienced in his own country and the fact that most Americans looked upon his ensemble as just another dance band. Luckily when touring the United States, the band had its own Pullman railroad car so the musicians could eat and sleep without incident.

In the early part of the 1930s, Ellington's ensemble recorded for Victor and Brunswick, staying with Brunswick exclusively from 1934 to 1940 (he left Victor when a recording producer used an ethnic slur during a recording session). Ellington also continued to add to his group of outstanding musicians.

"Ring Dem Bells" by Duke Ellington
e: RCA Victor Recording Studios, 1016 North Sycamore
Ave..ue, Los Angeles
When: August 26, 1930

With drummer Sonny Greer on chimes, this is another hot dance number written to feature Ellington's soloists. After a statement of the melody, clarinetist Barney Bigard has a solo (0:21), followed by alto saxophonist Johnny Hodges playing over the ensemble (0:37). Baritone saxophonist Harry Carney (0:53) and Joe "Tricky Sam" Nanton solo next (1:10). An unusual trade between Hodges and the scatting of Charles "Cootie" Williams follows, wherein Williams repeats what Hodges plays (1:26). The key changes with some hot chimes, and a solo by Williams follows, this time on trumpet (1:47). Saxes and chimes trade (2:20), and the full band plays a final time (2:37), ending in Greer's cymbals.

It was during the early 1930s when Ellington began presenting songs under his authorship that became standards and that the ensemble played for many years.

What: "Sophisticated Lady" by Duke Ellington, Irving Mills, and Mitchell Parish; arranged by Ellington
Where: Brunswick Recording Studios, 1776 Broadway, New York
When: May 16, 1933

One of Ellington's most popular songs, it is now known that the melody in the A section was actually written by trombonist Lawrence Brown, and the B section melody was composed by saxophonist Otto Hardwick. This was the second recording of the piece, which begins with a dramatic introduction, then the melody is played by Brown split with the trumpet of Artie Whetsel (0:15). The B section (or "release") brings us the clarinet of Barney Bigard (1:06), with Brown returning with the melody. Ellington plays a solo out of tempo, highly unusual for the time as these records were intended for dancing (on the first recording of "Sophisticated Lady," this section is played by harmonized saxes in tempo) (1:53). What follows is a rare Otto (pronounced Oh-toe) Hardwick alto saxophone solo (2:39) that lasts until the end of the record.

What: "Stompy Jones" by Duke Ellington
Where: RCA Victor Studios, 222 West North Bank Street, Suite 1143, Chicago
When: January 9, 1934

There really isn't melody to speak of, but since this book is about jazz and the role that legendary soloists had in making the big bands great, here is another solo feast!

After offbeat trumpet figures and trombonist Lawrence Brown answers, Barney Bigard (0:11), Williams (0:31), and Carney solo (0:49). Note the wa-wa trombone figures behind Carney. Brown returns with a full solo (1:09), and then trumpets trade figures with Ellington (1:28). The ensemble continues with Nanton (1:49) and Bigard soloing (2:06).

What: "Solitude" by Eddie DeLange, Irving Mills, and Duke Ellington; arranged by Ellington
Where: Brunswick Recording Studios, 1776 Broadway, New York
When: September 13, 1934

"Solitude" was first recorded for RCA on January 9, but the company didn't release it until after this recording came out. Ironically, both the RCA and the Brunswick sides sold well!

The melody is played by a beautiful instrumental color: clarinet, trumpet, and trombone both in cup mutes. The bridge features Carney's solo (0:49). The entire band plays the melody (1:36) until the end of the track. A very simple statement for a very profound and lovely song.

During this period, Ellington recorded his longest work to date, "Reminiscing in Tempo," which proved somewhat controversial, garnering both wildly enthusiastic and wildly denigrating reactions, typical of the reception of his concert music in the years to come.

In 1927, the Orange Blossoms, a Detroit-based orchestra managed by Jean Goldkette, completed an eight-month residency at the Casa Loma hotel in Toronto and took the name Casa Loma. The orchestra became a corporation in 1930, and all band members became shareholders, operating under strict rules. As a result, there was minimal turnover in the early years of the ensemble. Guitarist Gene Gifford was chief arranger for the orchestra, but he would be voted out of the group in 1935. Although many found the band to be over-rehearsed and rhythmically stiff, the ensemble had a national following during the early 1930s.

What: "Black Jazz" by Gene Gifford
Where: Brunswick Recording Studios, 1776 Broadway, New York
When: December 18, 1931

Casa Loma was a band that played both sweet and hot, and the combination made it a popular band at colleges in the early 1930s. Its "hot" music pointed the way to a new, exciting danceable style, and the band is now considered a bridge to the new swing music that was starting to be played by black bands. "Black Jazz" is a showcase for the band's soloists.

The melody of "Black Jazz" is a series of repeated "riffs" (or short melodic phrases). Soloists are trombonist Pee Wee Hunt (0:28), clarinetist Clarence Hutchinrider (1:17), trumpeter Grady Watts (1:41), and tenor saxophonist Pat Davis (2:05). The track is exciting and the soloists okay; it is an excellent example of how this nationally known ensemble showed off its jazz style. Casa Loma would continue to be a popular band even after the explosion of the swing era, modernizing its style and continuing to attract and retain excellent musicians.

Fletcher Henderson was still leading a first-class orchestra, even though bookings necessitated long trips in between jobs, with the band often arriving late. John Hammond was a jazz fan from a wealthy family who tried to help the band out (he would later "discover" Billie Holiday).

What: "Queer Notions" by Coleman Hawkins; arranged by Horace Henderson
Where: Columbia Studios, 55 Fifth Avenue, New York
When: September 22, 1933

Hammond arranged for the Henderson band to make some records for the European market. Saxophonist Coleman Hawkins wrote this unusual tune, which was arranged by Horace Henderson. It was not released in the United States until several years later. The piece certainly does not sound like a pop song of the time or the blues; harmonically, one could say it sounds like Debussy or Ravel meets the jazz orchestra.

Harmonized saxes play the melody after the introduction (0:12), which features Hawkins. Trumpeter Henry "Red" Allen solos over rhythmic patterns in the saxes (1:07), then Allen and Coleman solo back and forth against the unusual harmony (1:30). Hawkins has another brief solo after a statement by the full orchestra (2:11). Notice the powerful rhythm section of Bernard Addison on guitar, John Kirby on bass, and Walter Johnson on drums, which is beautifully recorded here.

John Hammond would suggest that Henderson arrange for a band led by a white clarinetist who had a national radio show. But Fletcher still had his own band for a time. Here he presents an updated arrangement of one of his big hits.

What: "Shanghai Shuffle" by Gene Rodemich and Larry Conley; arranged by Fletcher Henderson
Where: Decca Studios, 799 Seventh Avenue, New York
When: September 11, 1934

A new version of the classic 1920s arrangement, this opens with an introduction by the full band, the melody played by harmonized saxes (0:09), some variations of the tune with saxes and brass participating in a call and response (0:24), leading to a clarinet solo by William "Buster" Bailey (who once played duets with Benny Goodman when both were students) (1:28). Henry "Red" Allen plays a blistering solo (2:00) and the band continues with saxes and brass switching phrases (more call and response) and a brief Russell Procope solo (2:45).

Henderson finally disbanded in December 1934 and joined the clarinetist full time, but he would lead his own band again in the years ahead.

Among the territory bands, Alphonso Trent led one of the greatest. According to tenor saxophonist Budd Johnson, Trent worked the finest hotels in the South, always with excellent musicians, and the ensemble's music was years ahead of its time. Trent is a great example of why history suffers due to the many gaps in the historical record: there is very little left to show how great this band was except for a handful of recordings on the Gennett or Champion labels, which were not distributed well. Among them is a masterpiece.

What: "Clementine (from New Orleans)" by Henry Creamer and Harry Warren; arranged by Gus Wilson
Where: Gennett Studios, Richmond, Indiana
When: March 24, 1933

It's clear to me that arranger Wilson heard the Goldkette recording of this tune. He is clearly influenced by it, but it is not a copy as much as a tribute, because it goes its own way while reminding us of the original. After a short introduction, the melody is heard with embellishments by trumpeter Peanuts Holland (0:06), the ensemble takes over (0:27) with saxes featured (0:52) before the full ensemble returns (1:02). Trombonist Snub Mosley has a solo (1:14) before some harmonically advanced figures are heard in the ensemble (1:24). Trumpet soloist Harry "Sweets" Edison has a short solo (1:40). Notice how individual voices weave in and out for short periods as the ensemble continues. There is a key change (2:29) as the band continues to roar. Tenor saxophonist Hayes Pillars has a short solo (2:50) before the ensemble returns to end the record.

What we notice is the infectious, rock-steady rhythm of this organization under a well-rehearsed group of powerhouse musicians. Trent left music for a time in 1934, organizing another band in 1938. He died in 1959, leaving this tantalizing souvenir of one of the finest territory bands of the era.

Earl Hines was born in Duquesne, Pennsylvania, and was on the road as a piano accompanist for baritone Lois Deppe at the age of seventeen. He moved to Chicago in 1925 and was soon playing and recording with Louis Armstrong. By 1928, he was leading a band at the prestigious Grand Terrace Café, touring during the summers. His broadcasts were heard nationwide, and his style of performance influenced such future stars as Nat "King" Cole, Art Tatum, Jay McShann, and Stan Kenton. His gig at the Grand Terrace finally ended in 1940, but as we will see later, he led one of the most important bands of all time in 1943.

What: "Rosetta" by Earl Hines; arranged by Cecil Irwin
Where: Brunswick Recording Studios, Chicago
When: February 13, 1933

"Rosetta" was recorded twice on this date: once as an instrumental and once as a vocal. This is the instrumental version, which was not released until several years later. The melody is played by tenor and baritone saxes with trombone wa-was in the background (an effect created when a musician moves his or her hand inside to outside of the bell of the instrument) separated by a George Dixon improvised trumpet solo (0:27). Hines gets a full chorus, and it is a stunner, technically virtuosic, even going in and out of tempo (0:57). Alto saxophonist Omar Simeon (another musician from New Orleans) plays a full chorus with brass punctuations (1:56). Hines returns briefly (2:55) to end the recording.

The National Biscuit Company (Nabisco) wanted to promote their product, and the company's ad agency thought that the perfect medium was a dance music program on Saturday nights. On December 1, 1934, the *Let's Dance* program was on the air with three bands heard over the NBC Radio Network, one "sweet," one Latin, and one swing. The swing group was led by Benny Goodman, who'd started his own orchestra earlier in the year. Many listeners heard the new swing style for the first time. Something new was happening in American pop music, and would explode in the coming years.

4

THE EXPLOSION OF THE SWING ERA
1936–1942

After the cancellation of the *Let's Dance* program due to labor problems at Nabisco, agent Willard Alexander booked a nationwide tour for the Benny Goodman Orchestra. The tour did not go well as the band moved west, but Alexander told Goodman to keep going. Persistence paid off when the band played at the Palomar Ballroom on August 21, 1935. The first set was made up of "safe" music that the band played on the road when their swing repertoire was received with indifference or outright hostility. When the band finally cut loose, playing their most exciting pieces, the audience cheered and crowded around the bandstand. Many historians date the swing era as starting that night at the Palomar.

From that point on, the Goodman band was a solid hit wherever it played, staying six months at the Congress Hotel in Chicago (with broadcasts heard nationwide), returning to the West Coast to star in the movie *Hollywood Hotel* and playing the Palomar again. On June 30, 1936, the Goodman band became the house orchestra on the Camel Caravan radio program. Goodman was most fortunate to have the services of arrangers Fletcher Henderson, Lyle "Spud" Murphy, and Jimmy Mundy; Henderson adapted his own band's arrangements to Goodman's group, as well as writing many stunning new scores. Fletcher's brother Horace joined the arranging staff later and wrote some great scores in addition to completing some of Fletcher's work.

When the band headed back to New York, it was booked into the Paramount Theatre, where the band was part of a live presentation after the showing of a motion picture. On opening day, March 3, 1937, there was pandemonium in the theater, with teenagers dancing in the aisles and staying the entire day. Swing music was now the "hep" music style.

Happily, home recordists and ad agencies preserved a lot of live big band music from this period onward, unbeknownst to most of the musicians themselves. Some of the finest performances of the era are in active circulation, available both legally and illegally, and on Internet Web sites such as YouTube. Whenever possible, this book uses live performances as examples, as they are a far better representation of how the bands really sounded.

Let's start with the band that busted the swing era wide open!

What: "Ridin' High" by Cole Porter; arranged by Jimmy Mundy
Where: Camel Caravan Program, New York
When: November 2, 1937

This is how most people envision the swing era—the Benny Goodman band playing an up-tempo "killer-diller," as such a fast, exciting arrangement was called. The song is in AABA form. After a short introduction, the first chorus has the brass playing the melody and the saxes alternate with counter lines in another example of call and response (0:04). Goodman then takes a solo alternating with trumpeter Harry James (1:07), and his virtuosity is startling as the powerful rhythm section of pianist Jess Stacy, guitarist Allen Reuss, bassist Harry Goodman, and drummer Gene Krupa keep this incredibly fast tempo steady and exciting, almost like a swing machine. The entire ensemble finishes the piece with a key change and a paraphrase of the melody (2:10). This was the opener of the broadcast!

Like any other art form, the big bands had their share of mysteries, foul-ups, mistakes, and out-and-out disasters. Benny Goodman was involved in a group of recordings that proved somewhat embarrassing, resulting in a couple of records that have become collector's items.

Like many other musicians, Goodman admired Ella Fitzgerald and invited her to make some records. Someone should have thought about the fact that she was the singer for Chick Webb's Orchestra. . . .

What: "Goodnight My Love" by Mack Gordon and Harry Revel; arranged by Jimmy Mundy
Where: RCA Victor Studios, 145 East 24th Street, New York
When: November 6, 1936

This is a straightforward dance record of a song played through, a key change (1:21), a vocal (1:29), and a finish with Benny Goodman playing a short solo. But Ella being Ella, there's a jazzy turn of phrase (2:05) that clearly makes this special.

Decca Records threatened to sue when the recording was released, so RCA pulled it from the market. Not wanting to lose a potential hit record by the top band in the country, Goodman was asked to rerecord it with another vocalist.

What: "Goodnight My Love" by Mack Gordon and Harry Revel; arranged by Jimmy Mundy
Where: RCA Victor Studios, 145 East 24th Street, New York
When: January 14, 1937

Everything is the same except the vocal is now rendered by Frances Hunt, a perfectly professional singer, but not Ella Fitzgerald.

Listen to pianist Jess Stacy on both takes, a tasteful, creative accompanist whom singers loved. His accompaniment is totally different on each performance.

On January 16, 1938, Goodman's was the first popular dance orchestra to play Carnegie Hall, further cementing his orchestra's celebrity; happily, a recording was made by Albert Marx and is widely available. But key personnel such as James and Krupa left to form their own bands soon afterward. In 1939, Goodman knew that he needed a new musical direction and hired Eddie Sauter as chief arranger, one of the most innovative composer/arrangers of the twentieth century. Several excellent recordings resulted, but Goodman's own medical issues forced him to disband in July 1940.

Before that, Goodman switched from RCA Victor to the Columbia label, which had been purchased by the Columbia Broadcasting System.

What: "Just Like Taking Candy from a Baby" by Fred Astaire and Gladys Shelley; arranged by Fletcher Henderson
Where: World Broadcasting Studios, Los Angeles
When: April 30, 1940

Fred Astaire didn't make too many records in his incredible career, but his meeting with the Goodman band and the sextet is pure magic. The band plays the song, Astaire sings it (0:48) and then does a dance routine while the sextet accompanies him (1:28). There is a key change (2:03) and Goodman solos over the band with a brief solo by alto saxophonist Toots Mondello (2:18). Astaire returns to tap accompanied by the sextet, and the full band ends the track.

Benny put together a new band in October, and Sauter and several other musicians returned, including Charlie Christian, a member of Goodman's small groups who was one of the first to play an electric guitar. Christian would eventually take over the guitar chair in the full orchestra as well.

What: "Solo Flight" ("Chonk, Charlie, Chonk") by Charlie Christian, Benny Goodman, and Jimmy Mundy; arranged by Mundy
Where: Liederkrantz Hall, 111 East 58th Street, New York
When: March 4, 1941

This is a solo guitar feature for Christian and the Goodman Orchestra with a short solo by Goodman in the middle of the track (2:00). Christian's solo is a gem, a single-line bluesy solo that influenced the musicians who contributed to the modern jazz of the mid- to late 1940s called bebop (more about this later). Happily, an additional take is available from the studio session, which has been included as a link at the end of this book; several live performances are available as well. All of them are very different, and all of them are excellent.

Unfortunately, Christian did not live long enough to develop his considerable talent. He died of tuberculosis in 1942 at the age of twenty-five.

Another person who became a superstar joined the band in 1941 and stayed two years. Reportedly singer/songwriter Peggy Lee was unhappy with many of the songs she was asked to sing, and one day Goodman overheard her listening to a record of "Why Don't You Do Right," sung by Lil Green with Big Bill Broonzy accompanying on guitar. Benny asked if Peggy wanted to sing the song with the band, and she said she'd love to.

What: "Why Don't You Do Right?" by "Kansas" Joe McCoy; arranged by Mel Powell
Where: Liederkranz Hall, 111 East 58th Street, New York
When: July 27, 1942

Originally known as "Weed Smoker's Dream" when it was first written in 1936, McCoy added lyrics and it was recorded. The band plays an introduction with a brief solo by Goodman (0:12) and then the melody is heard simply, played in unison. Lee comes in with the vocal (0:37) and sings while Goodman or trumpeter Jimmy Maxwell fill in behind her at times. The band plays a chorus on its own, and then Goodman has an excellent solo, one of his best during this period (2:06). Lee returns to finish out the recording.

This recording became part of the Peggy Lee legend. Previously, she sounded somewhat scared and unsure of herself (John Hammond told Goodman she was terrible and suggested firing her), but here she blossoms, clearly enjoying the blues song and showing how good she was when the material was right for her. The record was a hit, and Lee later sang it in the motion picture *Stage Door Canteen* (a link can be found in "Recorded Sources and Further Listening" at the end of this book); she rerecorded the song in 1947.

On record dates as early as 1928, trombonist Tommy Dorsey co-led a band with his brother, clarinet and alto sax virtuoso Jimmy Dorsey (who was a great favorite of jazz legend Charlie Parker). By the mid-1930s, the Dorsey Brothers had a very popular touring dance orchestra staffed with excellent musicians; Glenn Miller played trombone and contributed many arrangements. But the Dorseys had a volatile relationship; one night Jimmy questioned a tempo set by front man Tommy. Tommy simply walked off the stand, quickly took over an orchestra led by Joe Haymes, and signed a recording contract with RCA Victor.

Several historians have said that Tommy Dorsey led the greatest all-around orchestra during the swing era. It could play ballads beautifully, it could swing, it had excellent soloists, great singers (one of whom was Frank Sinatra), and Tommy's trombone was one of the most distinctive musical voices of the entire era, a model for trombonists all over the world (even French Horn virtuoso Dennis Brain was a huge fan). Dorsey also played trumpet but rarely with his band.

What: "Stop, Look and Listen" by Ralph Freed and John and George Van Eps; arranged by Glenn Miller; adapted by Deane Kincaide
Where: RCA Victor Studios, 145 East 24th Street, New York
When: April 5, 1937

Most popular recordings were ten inches in diameter, usually holding no more than three-and-a-half minutes per side. Only on rare occasions were big band recordings released on twelve inch records, the size reserved for concert music. "Stop, Look and Listen" was not only issued as a twelve-inch record, but it was part of an album of twelve inchers that included Benny Goodman's anthem of the swing era, "Sing, Sing, Sing."

Using an old arrangement written by Glenn Miller and first recorded for Decca on August 15, 1934, this recording is mostly a showcase for the great soloists in the Dorsey band. The first chorus is the same as the older record (saxes in unison with brass punctuations for the two A sections, brass on the B section, repeat of the A section), but once the solos kick in, this is a brand-new experience. Tommy has the first solo (0:55), Pee Wee Erwin the second on trumpet (1:41) with trombones playing a background figure. Notice the trombones play the same background with cup mutes toward the end of the solo, a nice contrast (2:17). Johnny Mince solos on clarinet next with brass playing a different background this time (2:27). Tenor saxophonist Bud Freeman plays an excellent solo, which begins in stop time (3:14). Freeman had played with Tommy as early as the 1920s and was considered an important soloist in small groups; his being a Dorsey sideman was a real coup for the leader. Freeman gets an additional chorus featuring one figure repeated with brass and drum punctuations. The A section melody returns after Freeman ends his solo (4:48), backed by brass "stinging" figures in straight mutes, with Dorsey taking another solo in the B section, this time in a straight mute (5:00). The recording ends as the melody quietly finishes. That's a solid five-and-a-half minutes of pure, danceable jazz with great solos.

When you listen to this track, pay particular attention to the drums of Dave Tough, another musician who'd been playing and recording since the late 1920s. At the beginning of this recording, he plays woodblocks on beats two and four then switches to full drum set. His drumming behind Mince's solo is particularly exciting, flashy without stealing the spotlight from Mince's clarinet, and his beat is rock steady. Tough was beloved by musicians and played with many of the top bands during the swing era led by Artie Shaw, Benny Goodman, and Woody Herman. He would die much too young at the age of forty-one.

Artie Shaw was a busy clarinetist and saxophonist in the radio and recording studios when he was invited to participate in an all-star swing music concert in May 1936 at the Imperial Theatre in New York. His "Interlude in B ♭" was scored for clarinet, string quartet, and rhythm section, and it was so well received that he repeated it for an encore because he had nothing else prepared. Almost overnight, he was pursued by booking agents who wanted him to form his own band. Against his better judgment, Shaw did just that, but from the outset it was clear that he would do things his way. His first band was made up of clarinet, tenor sax, two trumpets, trombone, string quartet, and rhythm section. The band recorded for the Brunswick label, and one of the best recordings of this early Shaw band was "Cream Puff," composed by Franklyn Marks, whom Shaw claimed was one of the few writers who understood how he wanted the band to sound.

What: "Cream Puff" by Franklyn Marks
Where: Brunswick Recording Studios, 1776 Broadway, New York
When: December 23, 1936

"Cream Puff" is a freewheeling swing piece with a sound reminiscent of a combo: Shaw plays melody and the brass play behind him with saxes and strings providing a "pad" (instruments playing in harmony)—they are "felt" more than heard, but theirs is a distinctive sound unlike anything else being heard at the time (0:08). A nice touch is a string pizzicato section under the melody in three spots (1:23, 2:10, and at the very end). Joe Lipman plays a solo on piano backed by small-group veteran George Wettling playing on the rim of his drums (1:26). This record also has one of the earliest examples of Shaw soloing with drums alone, an element that would become part of many Shaw arrangements (2:12). Overall, this is an exciting recording, but the band's sound was not loud enough to fill large ballrooms, and ballroom owners complained to Artie and his management. With great reluctance, Shaw was forced to disband.

He then put together a standard big band of the time made up of four saxophones, three trumpets, two (later three) trombones, guitar, piano, bass, and drums. A new record contract with the RCA Victor budget label Bluebird in July 1938 resulted in his first hit on his first session for the label, "Begin the Beguine." The song had been written by Cole Porter for a 1935 show called "Jubilee" but didn't become popular at the time due to its length. Shaw liked it and recorded it as a B side of a single and was as surprised as anyone that the song not only became a hit, but subsequently one of the greatest hits of the swing era.

What: "Begin the Beguine," by Cole Porter; arranged by Jerry Gray
Where: RCA Victor Studios, 145 East 24th Street, New York
When: July 24, 1938

In preparing the arrangement, Gray let the song basically play itself with Shaw's clarinet as the lead voice at the beginning, end, and interspersed throughout the recording. Shaw plays the melody straight for the first A section (0:06), then harmonized saxes take over with brass punctuations for the second A (0:34). The entire band plays the bridge, leading to a tenor sax solo played by Tony Pastor (1:28). The band then takes over the melody (with a short solo by Shaw) (1:52), but at the end of the arrangement, Shaw plays the final part of the melody and then a lip slur (a technique where the pitch slides from low to high by altering the mouth's grip on the mouthpiece) (2:56), leading to the final notes played into the highest range of the clarinet as the band plays a final figure.

Shaw's world changed completely—he was now besieged by music publishers, reporters, and overenthusiastic fans whose actions disgusted him. After walking out on the band and taking a short vacation in Latin America, Artie Shaw went back into the recording studio to make some new records. Since he didn't have a band of his own, he hired freelancers and recorded some songs he'd heard while on vacation. One of these, "Frenesi," became a huge hit, and although he resisted it, he returned to the band business, this time with a full string section. Disbanding yet again in 1941, he put together his largest orchestra in September.

What: "Just Kiddin' Around" by Ray Conniff
Where: RCA Victor Studios, 222 North Bank Street, Suite 1143, Chicago
When: October 30, 1941

This is another great example of a simple riff melody as a perfect excuse to feature soloists. After a short piano solo played by Johnny Guarnieri, the melody is introduced and repeated with brass accentuations (0:12). Shaw takes over with a playful solo with string harmony in the background (0:36). Then Hot Lips Page plays a burning chorus on trumpet with a cup mute (1:01). Saxes play a harmonized chorus (1:27). Brass play wa-was behind Georgie Auld's tenor solo (1:53), with Shaw returning for more solo space, saxes playing a riff behind him (2:19). The full band takes over in a different key until the end (2:43). Listen to how the strings fill in behind the roaring saxes and brass.

Shaw was another leader who had African American musicians in his band, in this case Oran "Hot Lips" Page. Benny Goodman had pianist

Teddy Wilson and vibraharpist Lionel Hampton as part of his small group in 1936 (although they did not play with the full band until later); a white bandleader touring with a mixed-race band remained controversial for several years. Such ensembles faced discrimination and insults from patrons in different parts of the country, so only the most successful bandleaders dared to try it. But Shaw didn't care, hosting Billie Holiday as the band's singer for a while. As we see in the next chapter, he would later host trumpeter Roy Eldridge.

Jimmie Lunceford had been a student of music in Denver, Colorado, with Wilberforce Whiteman, Paul Whiteman's father. Graduating from Fisk University, he became the athletic director and band instructor at Manassas High School in Memphis, Tennessee in 1927, and was perhaps the first instructor to teach jazz at a public school in the United States. In 1929 Lunceford assembled a band made up of his students who turned professional, and by 1934 they were playing at the prestigious Cotton Club in New York City. This would be the first black band to tour colleges and universities throughout the country. The Lunceford band was one of the most musically and visually exciting bands of the swing era and was a big influence on Glenn Miller, who adapted the band's showmanship (waving mutes, dancing, hip hand gestures) to his band. Happily, the band made a short film in 1936 for Warner Bros. A YouTube link of it can be found in "Recorded Sources and Further Listening" at the end of this book so that you can see the band in action.

Its chief arranger was Melvin "Sy" Oliver, who established its musical style, a two-beat bouncy approach (bass plays on one and three, a style that was considered old-fashioned by the mid-1930s but proved infectious when the Lunceford band played it).

What: "My Blue Heaven" by Walter Donaldson and George Whiting; arranged by Sy Oliver
Where: Decca Recording Studios, 799 Seventh Avenue, New York
When: December 23, 1935

An out-of-tempo introduction by pianist Ed Wilcox leads to an exciting brass fanfare. The melody is paraphrased by unison saxes (0:14), which makes the music sound like it is being made up on the spot. Notice the bass on one and three played by Mose Allen. After a brief transition by tenor saxophonist Joe Thomas (1:00), Willie Smith plays an improvised counter line on baritone sax against the band playing the melody in harmony (1:11); in between is another solo by Wilcox (1:34). Another transition by trombonist Russell Bowles announces a key change (1:55), another brass fanfare with sax fill (2:07), and then a vocal trio singing a hip version of the lyrics (2:19). A brief ending finishes this classic record, one of the recordings usually cited as a classic of swing style.

What: "Baby, Won't You Please Come Home?" by Charles Warfield and Clarence Williams (note: Warfield claimed he wrote the song himself); arranged by Sy Oliver
Where: American Recording Corp. Studios, 1776 Broadway, New York
When: January 31, 1939

Many historians cite this recording as one of the finest big band sides of the era. The musicians start out playing this 1919 standard in small-group Dixieland style, then the band kicks in with the rhythm in the modern style (0:31). A solo by tenor saxophonist Joe Thomas is backed by trombones (0:56). The band creates a long change with an assist by alto saxophonist Willie Smith (1:39), which leads to a hip vocal by Thomas (1:54), who takes the piece almost to the end, when Jimmy Crawford's drums and the band finish (2:42).

Lunceford's continued to be one of the most popular bands of that time. His musicians remained loyal to him despite grueling tour schedules and low pay, but many left by the early 1940s either because of the draft or because they had better opportunities elsewhere (Sy Oliver left in 1939 when Tommy Dorsey offered him $5,000 a year more). The replacements were good, but the spirit of the band was never the same. Lunceford hung on until he died suddenly under mysterious circumstances in 1947. The band continued for a time under the duel leadership of pianist Ed Wilcox and tenor saxophonist Joe Thomas, but they gave up in 1949.

Duke Ellington and Irving Mills ended their business relationship in mid-1939, and Ellington signed with the William Morris Agency. In 1940, he changed record labels, and many of his RCA Victor records between the years 1940 and 1942 are considered masterpieces. Two musicians in particular distinguish this version of the Ellington orchestra: Ben Webster, who was already considered one of the great tenor saxophonists in jazz, and bassist Jimmie Blanton, who changed the role of the bass, playing virtuoso musical lines, often at lightning speed, with an unmistakably full, rich sound, while keeping steady rhythm and swing. This edition of Ellington's ensemble has been called the Blanton-Webster Band.

What: "Ko-Ko" by Duke Ellington
Where: RCA Victor Studios, 222 N. West Bank Street, Suite 1143, Chicago
When: March 6, 1940

Drums, Harry Carney's baritone, and trombones playing an introduction bring us one of the most famous recordings in the history of American music, the composition an ominous-sounding minor blues unlike anything heard before. Juan Tizol plays the melody on valve trombone as a series of four-note phrases as saxes respond (once again, the idea of call and response is present in a big band piece) (0:12). Tricky Sam Nanton plays a solo with a cup mute and plunger going in and out of the horn imitating a human voice, as saxes play a different four-note figure and trumpets play a rhythmic pattern against it (0:31). Ellington solos, sounding percussive and harmonically dissonant (1:07). Full band can be heard next, with unison trumpets in plunger mutes answered by saxes and brass (1:25). The band and the bass trade four-bar phrases in the next chorus, and we can hear the power and beauty of Blanton's bass (1:44). For the last chorus, loud brass chords sound as the saxes play an accompanying figure (2:02), the intro is repeated (2:21), and then a spectacular ending by the entire band is heard, building up to a final, loud chord ending the recording.

As stated in chapter 3, Ellington wrote features to show off his musicians.

What: "Jack the Bear" by Duke Ellington
Where: RCA Victor Studios, 222 N. West Bank Street, Suite 1143, Chicago
When: March 6, 1940

It's now hard to imagine how innovative and shocking this recording was. Musicians across the world marveled at the incredible finger work and huge sound Blanton could produce on the string bass. During the recording, a soloist or the band itself plays a melody, only to be answered by Blanton; the recording features clarinetist Barney Bigard (0:37 and 1:02), trumpeter Cootie Williams (0:50), baritone saxophonist Harry Carney (1:33), and "Tricky Sam" Nanton (1:51).

Blanton's approach to the instrument would become standard rather quickly—a steady rhythmic foundation interspersed with virtuosic solos like a horn player or a guitarist.

Ellington had also taken on a composer/arranger whom he met in Pittsburgh. Billy Strayhorn would prove to be invaluable to Ellington, arranging pop tunes and also composing unique, beautiful compositions.

What: "Chelsea Bridge" by Billy Strayhorn
Where: RCA Victor Studios, Hollywood
When: December 2, 1941

A piano solo by the composer opens this beautiful instrumental that sounds like danceable concert music. It's been called impressionistic, reflecting the music of Claude Debussy and Maurice Ravel. The melody is played by soft brass (0:09), with a beautiful Ben Webster solo in the B section (0:47). After another short piano solo (1:27), saxes play a solo based on the melody, which is repeated (1:30). A solo by valve trombonist Juan Tizol (2:09) leads to a final restatement of the A section (2:28), which ends the recording.

"Chelsea Bridge" became a jazz standard played by many groups over the years, but this recording has never been matched with regard to mood, sound, gentle swing, and Strayhorn's virtuosic piano fills. In the opinion of many, including me, this is one of the most beautiful recordings ever made regardless of musical style.

When Strayhorn accompanied the Ellington ensemble on their various tours, this piece would be one of his features.

This was the beginning of the Ellington Orchestra charting a whole new course for big bands and American music. Although Duke and company continued to play dances and nightclubs, he aspired for his orchestra to become a concert attraction, and in 1943, he played the first of a series of concerts in Carnegie Hall.

Chick Webb was born in Baltimore, Maryland, and took up the drums as therapy when he contracted tuberculosis of the spine. Yet this short-statured, hunchbacked man was a drum powerhouse who influenced virtuoso drummers Gene Krupa and Buddy Rich. From 1931, Webb's band was the house ensemble at the Savoy Ballroom on 596 Lenox Avenue in the Harlem section of New York City, where the best dancers showed off in front of patrons. The ballroom could accommodate four thousand people and often sponsored "battles" between bands.

In 1934, at the nearby Apollo Theatre, a young girl won the Wednesday night amateur contest singing two songs and was recommended to Webb. He was reluctant to take her on, but the musicians in the band loved her, and her "audition," a dance at Yale University, was very successful. Ella Fitzgerald soon became one of the top vocalists in American music.

What: "Undecided" by Sid Robin and Charlie Shavers; arranged by Van Alexander
Where: Decca Studios, 50 West 57th Street, New York
When: February 17, 1939

After an introduction, the band plays the A section of the melody (0:10); after a key change (0:18), Ella takes over and it's her show (0:23). At the age of twenty-two, she already sounds assured, singing with great swing and improvisational-sounding changes to the melody. After a full chorus, the band really swings out with call and response between the brass and the saxes (1:45). There's a short tenor sax solo by Teddy McRae (2:00), and before Ella reenters, Webb shows off his tremendous power and technique in a short drum solo (2:18).

Webb passed away on June 16, 1939. Ella took over leadership of the band until 1942, when she started her solo career.

Count Basie was born in Red Bank, New Jersey, and had considerable playing experience in New York by the time he became the pianist of the Bennie Moten band in Kansas City, Missouri. When Moten died in 1935, Basie took some of Moten's musicians and formed his own band. Basie's brand of Midwest swing was infectious, and one night jazz enthusiast and writer John Hammond heard the band from the Reno Club via shortwave radio. He went to Kansas City to hear this new assemblage for himself and was soon raving about it in the music press. It wasn't long before the band was signed to Decca Records and came to New York. Its first gigs revealed that the band needed some further refining, but substitutions were made, and soon it was one of the most exciting ensembles in popular music.

This was yet another band made up of musicians who became legendary. The band boasted two tenor saxophonists who had totally different styles: Herschel Evans was a student of the aggressive Coleman Hawkins style of playing, Lester Young a pioneer of the "cooler" approach to the instrument, which was lighter sounding and more harmonically sophisticated, a style widely imitated by jazz musicians in the bebop era and beyond. Young was nicknamed "Prez" by Billie Holiday, short for president. Buck Clayton and later Harry "Sweets" Edison were trumpet soloists (Edison later became one of Frank Sinatra's favorite jazz soloists), and Dicky Wells soloed on trombone. The rhythm section of Freddie Green on guitar, the Count on piano, Walter Page on bass, and Jo Jones on drums became so famous and influential that it was later called the "All-American Rhythm Section."

The bulk of the band's first music library was what are known as "head arrangements," in which the music is made up on the bandstand and the musicians just keep adding to it. Although the band would later play arrangements of pop songs to compete in the music market, it still often sounded as if the music was being made up on the spot.

What: "Time Out" by Ed Durham
Where: Decca Recording Studios, 50 West 57th Street, New York
When: August 9, 1937

From the very first beat, this track swings powerfully yet subtly. There's really no melody to speak of, just a basic riff and harmonic background, an excuse for an audience to dance and the musicians to take solos. This is the type of piece that was often played for many minutes with lots of solo room.

Listen to the introduction in the saxes; you hear it throughout, as it serves as a transition to the next section of the arrangement (0:07). Something very unusual happens in the beginning of the recording, as Herschel Evans has a short solo (0:13), immediately followed by Lester Young with a longer solo (0:18). Only if you listen carefully can you hear one musician substituting for another. After Young finishes, we hear the introduction again, followed by a trumpet solo by Buck Clayton (0:54). Durham plays a short solo on electric guitar (one of the first electric guitar solos on record) (1:19), the introduction appears again, and then the Count gets a solo (1:34). Basie had prodigious technique, but he chose to use few notes and simple chords in his solos. The key changes (2:18) and the ensemble takes over with what serves as a melody in the brass and a counter line in the saxes. The introduction reappears, ending the recording (2:50), with the Count getting a last bass note in.

Along with Ellington and Jimmie Lunceford, the Basie band became incredibly popular with both black and white audiences. Basie had Billie Holiday as band vocalist for a time and always attracted excellent soloists and arrangers. By 1940, the orchestra had come a long way from its Kansas City beginnings and was touring all over the country.

What: "Broadway" by Henri Woode
Where: Liederkrantz Hall, 111 East 58th Street, New York
When: November 19, 1940

After a swinging, fanfare-like introduction featuring a short trumpet solo by Harry "Sweets" Edison, the melody in the A section is heard in the saxes (0:17) followed by a solo by the Count for the B section (0:38).

After a repeat of the A section (0:48), Lester Young delivers a one-chorus solo that has become a classic (1:01). This was his last session with this version of the Basie Orchestra and he would be missed. Edison returns (1:41) and there's a call and response between brass and saxes based on the introduction (2:03). Count returns for a solo (2:25), and the melody returns (2:34), becoming softer on the repeat until the piece ends with brass punctuations.

We visit with Count and crew later.

Like Jimmie Lunceford, Andy Kirk had been a student of Paul Whiteman's father Wilberforce in Denver, Colorado. Kirk was a member of a band in Dallas, Texas, led by Terrence Holder called Dark Clouds of Joy. When Kirk became the band's leader, he relocated it to Kansas City, Kansas, and renamed it Clouds of Joy. He made some records from 1929 to 1930 but is most known for the ensemble that recorded for Decca beginning in 1936. For several years, Clouds of Joy were a top band playing in the loose, swinging Kansas City style.

Although the band boasted several wonderful soloists over the years, the main attraction was the band's pianist, arranger, and composer Mary Lou Williams, one of the few women who was a regular member of a big band. Her compositions, arrangements, and piano solos are among the highlights of the swing era.

What: "Walkin' and Swingin'" by Mary Lou Williams
Where: Decca Studios, 799 Seventh Avenue, New York
When: March 2, 1936

The first recording the band made for Decca, this piece is in AABA form, with saxes playing the melody against brass, brass taking over in the B section (0:20), and the A section slightly modified, taking us into a new key (0:42) and a chorus of trumpets and reeds playing a modification and elaboration of the melody. Mary Lou plays a solo on piano (1:22), split with Dick Wilson on tenor sax with brass behind him. The full band finishes by playing a variation on the melody for the last chorus (1:59) with a section of trumpets and saxes calling and responding (note the humorous reference to the song "The Peanut Vendor" during this section).

Williams later became a composer of symphonic and religious music and an early champion of the musicians playing the new bebop style in the mid-1940s.

Red Norvo was a virtuoso xylophonist in vaudeville when he joined the Paul Whiteman Orchestra in 1932, marrying the band's vocalist Mildred Bailey. He subsequently co-led a band with saxophonist Charlie Barnet before starting his own in 1936 with Bailey; they became known as Mr. and Mrs. Swing. Like Artie Shaw's first ensemble, Norvo created a group that sounded intimate and could not be heard when playing large ballrooms; after all, a xylophone was not a loud instrument to begin with. But their swing was infectious and loved by musicians, especially when Bailey sang. Eddie Sauter wrote the arrangements and played trumpet.

What: "Smoke Dreams" by Arthur Freed and Nacio Herb Brown; arranged by Eddie Sauter
Where: Brunswick Recording Studios, 666 Lake Shore Drive, Chicago
When: January 8, 1937

Reportedly written when Sauter was angry at Bailey (Mildred had an explosive personality and was continually pushing the musicians to swing more), this arrangement is harmonically complex and almost surreal; it's truly a wonder that Brunswick released it. Bailey gets help with her first note by pianist Joe Liss giving it to her (0:16) and then sails through the ensemble's harmonic wandering perfectly. After Mildred sings a full chorus of the song, the band takes over with more strange sounds (1:28), broken up by trumpet soloist Stu Pletcher (2:00). The band continues until the end, when Liss ends with a strange chord, wrapping up the proceedings.

This recording became an instant classic among musicians, but like Artie Shaw, Norvo would disband and organize a louder orchestra in 1938.

Glenn Miller had been a well-respected trombonist and arranger as early as the mid-1920s, first with Ben Pollack's Orchestra, then with

Red Nichols. In 1934, he worked with the Dorsey Brothers band, assembled an all-star ensemble for British arranger Ray Noble's first American band, and formed an ensemble of his own in 1937, recording for Brunswick. His famous trademark of five reeds with clarinet on top of four saxophones was already in place, but this first band failed. Although he lost a lot of money, Miller decided to try again a few months later. Vocalists Marion Hutton (Betty Hutton's sister) and Ray Eberle were not great singers, but they were charming and personable and the public loved them. Tenor saxophonist Gordon "Tex" Beneke was a good soloist who also sang well. Miller led a band that was "sweet" (listen to his monster hit "Moonlight Serenade"—those reeds were indeed seductive), but included just enough powerful swing to keep dancers excited. Although he admired Count Basie and Jimmie Lunceford, Miller was careful to always appeal to the general listener, and his instincts were usually right.

Miller was responsible for the recording that became the anthem of the swing era, "In the Mood." This piece has an interesting history. The simple theme of a repeated phrase in the reeds was originally heard on a recording from 1930 by trumpet player Wingy Manone called "Tar Paper Stomp." A few months later, Horace Henderson included the same riff in a composition recorded by Fletcher Henderson's band named "Hot and Bothered." Saxophonist Joe Garland heard it and reused it, added to it, and called his creation "In the Mood." Originally this piece was given to Edgar Hayes, Gene Krupa, and Artie Shaw, all of whom liked it and played it, but a live broadcast by the Shaw Orchestra reveals that Shaw played it too slowly and that the piece had too many ideas and a weak ending. Garland then brought it to Miller, who sensed that it was a hit but needed some cutting and shaping to get it onto a record and ultimately to make it memorable. Before the arrangement was finalized, he played the entire version a few times, and a broadcast exists, running over four minutes.

What: "In the Mood" by Joe Garland
Where: Glen Island Casino, Shore Road and Route 1-A, New
Rochelle, New York
When: July 26, 1939

In order to understand how this piece was transformed into a huge hit, let's look at the form of the original: introduction; theme (repeated) (0:32); second strain (repeated) (1:04); transition one (1:25); third strain (repeated) (1:28); transition two (1:50); third strain (2:01); tenor sax solo (2:12); transition three (2:34); second tenor sax solo (2:45); transition four (trumpet section) (2:55); trumpet solo (repeated) (3:01); transition five (3:22); theme repeated three to four times, getting softer each time (3:25); theme repeated loudly (4:38); trumpet "fanfare" leading to ending (4:52).

Based on interviews, Miller, Eddie Durham, and band pianist "Chummy" MacGregor are credited with the arrangement in its final form.

This live performance indicates that to create the hit version, Miller sped up the tempo slightly to a lively, exciting swing perfect for dancing. He cut the second strain and the transition afterward, kept the third strain (the call and response between the saxes and trumpets), and repeated it, cut out transition two and the additional repeat of the third strain, condensed the tenor solos (now this is a "duel" between Tex Beneke and Al Klink), and then played the rest of the arrangement as is. He wisely focused on the main theme, cutting out two other themes that were weaker.

What: "In the Mood" by Joe Garland; final version by Eddie
Durham, Glenn Miller, and Chummy MacGregor
Where: RCA Victor Studios, 145 East 24th Street, New York
When: August 1, 1939

This is what we have left: introduction; theme (repeated) (0:11); third strain (repeated) (0:45); tenor sax solos (one chorus) (1:07), transition four (1:31); trumpet solo (1:36); transition five (2:00); theme repeated softer and softer (2:03), theme repeated loudly (3:01), "fanfare" leading into finish (3:16).

Needless to say, this became the band's biggest hit, and somewhere in the world at any given time, "In the Mood" can be heard on radio, television, or played by professional and amateur bands alike.

When 1940 began, Glenn Miller was considered by many to be the top bandleader in the nation. He was quick to tell those interested that he considered himself a businessman first, and the band was run like a corporation, everything carefully planned to appeal to the widest audience possible. The band appeared on a radio show for Chesterfield cigarettes three times a week plus unsponsored broadcasts from venues where they were playing, and they did sellout business.

One of Miller's chief arrangers was the brilliant Bill Finegan, one of the great composers of the twentieth century. Miller cut and edited Bill's music continually to get it down to "our" style, as he would say, but he admired Finegan tremendously. Finegan supplied some of the loveliest music of the era, as well as some swing classics, including his adaptation of "Song of the Volga Boatman." This arrangement of a Russian folk song is still played.

What: "Song of the Volga Boatman;" arranged by Bill Finegan
Where: RCA Victor Studios, 145 East 24th Street, New York
When: January 17, 1941

The piece begins with an ominous bass line in minor. Trombones have the melody in the A section of the song (0:17), and the melody is repeated with a Billy May cup-muted trumpet solo and sax background (notice Finegan does not use the clarinet lead sound here) (0:32). The B section is played by harmonized brass with sax background (0:48), followed by a repeated A section featuring stop time in which the rhythm doesn't play in a consistent pattern (Miller always reminded Finegan to keep the beat going, whereas Finegan said that dancers were smarter than that and would feel it regardless—this time Bill won) (1:03). A saxophone section transition leads to an alto saxophone solo by Ernie Caceres (who had been playing baritone up until now and switches for the solo—Caceres rarely, if ever, soloed on the large horn in the Miller band) (1:20); the solo is backed by brass punctuations: trumpets in mutes, trombones playing wa-was. Another transition leads to a drum solo (1:56), then something ingenious happens: the rhythm instruments drop out and a hand-clapping pattern is "played" under a fugue between the trumpets and trombones (2:05). After two big chords, saxes play a double-time figure (2:47), leading to the entire band playing the ending with an exciting conclusion.

This arrangement perfectly illustrates why Miller was so popular. A familiar song, a beat perfect for dancing, and an arrangement beautifully structured and realized for repeated listening.

There were other ensembles that came out of Kansas City during this period. Jay McShann was a local pianist who put together a big band that made several great recordings for Decca, and sitting in the saxophone section was a young man who would be one of the prime movers in modern jazz, Charles (Charlie) Parker.

What: "Hootie Blues" (Hootie was McShann's nickname) by Jay McShann and Charles Parker
Where: Dallas, Texas
When: April 30, 1941

Except for a short piano solo by McShann and an alto solo by Parker, this is a feature for blues shouter Walter Brown. But the solo by Parker is an important milestone in the history of jazz (0:35). He was twenty years old when he made this recording, and this solo has been transcribed and studied for many years, recognized as a groundbreaking musical statement that pointed toward the modern jazz that evolved in the coming years that came to be known as bop or bebop. Listen for the rhythmic variety and virtuosity of Parker's solo and his clear bell-like sound, which is actually somewhat subdued here.

Harlan Leonard was a saxophonist in Kansas City who co-led an ensemble with Thamon Hayes. When that ensemble broke up, he formed a new ensemble called Harlan Leonard and His Rockets. Much of the band's repertoire was made up of some form of the blues, but the band's recording of the pop song "I Don't Want to Set the World on Fire" was quite popular. One of the band's arrangers would later become a star in his own right as a composer and arranger; he'd already written for Count Basie and later wrote for Dizzy Gillespie.

What: "Rock and Ride" by Harlan Leonard and Tadd Dameron; arranged by Dameron
Where: RCA Victor Studios, 222 N. West Bank Street, Suite 1143, Chicago
When: July 15, 1940

After an introduction by saxes and trombones repeating the bass on offbeats, this piece explodes in sound (0:09) before saxes play the simple melody of the A section backed by brass playing wa-was (0:12). The B section is unison brass playing a bluesy line against sax harmonies (0:32) and then a repeat of the A (0:43). A brief fanfare-like transition in brass (0:53) leads to two trumpet players splitting a solo between them, James Ross and William Smith (0:57). Henry Bridges plays a tenor sax solo with brass background (1:40). The remainder of the recording is interesting: after the solo, the band plays two different variations of the A melody with saxes and brass interweaving (2:22). The B section features full band and drums trading (drummer Jesse Price would later have quite a career in California) (2:43), then another variation of the A section by the full band (2:53). The original A section is briefly repeated with a short, surprising ending played by saxes and trombones in unison (3:04).

Leonard's band is not as well-known as the other Kansas City big bands discussed in this chapter. Not only was it an exciting unit, but it allows us to hear Dameron's early writing. Leonard would leave music a few years later to work for the Internal Revenue Service until his retirement.

Singer and dancer Cab Calloway took over a band called the Missourians in 1930 and later played at the Cotton Club when the Ellington band was on tour. He was the main star as vocalist and entertainer, but his ensemble would have many important soloists such as tenor saxophonist Chu Berry and bassist Milt Hinton. In 1939, a young trumpeter and arranger named John Birks Gillespie joined the trumpet section and wrote arrangements as well.

What: "Pickin' the Cabbage" by John Birks "Dizzy" Gillespie
Where: Columbia Recording Studios, Chicago
When: March 8, 1940

This original piece is highlighted by an insinuating musical line in lower saxes and bass, leading to a clarinet and muted trumpet section duet on the A section (0:21), with the full band playing the B section (0:41). An unusual sounding full-chorus solo by Gillespie follows, filled with notes that sound wrong but become right as Gillespie resolves them (1:02). Full band takes over (1:43), but here again composer Gillespie does not do the easy thing, which would have been to have everyone play the same musical figures—he has the sax, trumpet (open by now), and trombone sections all playing something different as a counterpoint to each other. The melody is repeated (2:08), that insinuating line becomes softer and softer, and a drum break by Cozy Cole brings the band back for a final restatement as the track ends.

Calloway recognized Gillespie's talent but disliked his solo style. Gillespie was a practical joker as well, and was later blamed for shooting spitballs at Calloway as he performed on stage. Cab fired him, but Gillespie was not unemployed for long. He wrote for other bands and started an innovative small group. We revisit him in a few pages.

This chapter ends with the orchestra led by Benny Carter, who'd put together the ensemble for the Spike Hughes recording featured in chapter 3. Carter grew up in New York City and learned both the alto sax and the trumpet; he is one of those rare musicians who became a pioneering soloist playing instruments from two different instrumental families. A veteran of the Charlie Johnson and Fletcher Henderson orchestras, he became the musical director of McKinney's Cotton Pickers when Don Redman left. By the mid-1930s, he was one of most respected musicians in the country and led a big band with the top musicians in New York; it was said that to play with Carter was to reach the very top in the black music world. He left for Europe in 1935, arranged for the BBC Dance Orchestra under the direction of Henry Hall, and recorded and concertized with groups all over Europe. Among his recording personnel were Coleman Hawkins, who was also working in Europe at the time, and legendary Gypsy guitarist Django Reinhardt.

Returning in 1938, he formed a new orchestra and played at the Savoy Ballroom while writing arrangements for other bands. Irving Mills managed him briefly, and Carter recorded for Mills's label Master, released by OKeh/Vocalion.

What: "Sleep" by Earl Leibig; arranged by Benny Carter
Where: World Broadcasting System Studios, 711 Fifth Avenue, New York
When: January 30, 1940

In order to follow along closely with this recording, a very fast rendition of a piece that was originally a waltz and Fred Waring and his Pennsylvanians' theme, I break it down by choruses:

First chorus (0:06)—This song is in ABAC form. After a short introduction by pianist Eddie Heywood and the rhythm section, saxes play melody with brass fills.

Second chorus (0:32)—The key changes abruptly with the ensemble playing the paraphrased melody. Guest Coleman Hawkins solos during the B section and completes the chorus.

Transition (0:57)—Brass sound a fanfare-like phrase and trade with saxes.

Third chorus (1:06)—Eddie Heywood solos; saxes play long notes as brass play short figures.

Fourth chorus (1:31)—Another abrupt key change and we hear the trumpet of Joe Thomas soloing during the A and B sections of the song. Saxes and brass alternate figures and then Keg Purnell has a short drum solo.

Fifth chorus (1:56)—The key changes abruptly again, and after the full band plays, Carter takes a solo with band background.

Sixth chorus (2:20)—Brass and saxes alternate, trombones have a solo spot very high in their register, the band comes down in volume, building up to a held bass in which saxes and brass alternate the same figures (2:44) with full band finishing this exciting recording.

What Carter does here results in a masterpiece of arranging and performance by changing the waltz to an up-tempo "flag-waver" and then finding different ways to paraphrase the melody while building in solos. This arrangement is still as fresh as when it was first recorded.

Carter's band never had the success that Basie's and Ellington's had, as he never had a hit and was not the kind of flamboyant trumpet or alto sax soloist to become a star in the eyes of the public. But professionals knew that he was a musician's musician, so he never lacked for work. A job at 20th Century-Fox for the film *Stormy Weather* so impressed musical director Alfred Newman that Carter became a well-known composer and arranger for motion pictures, one of the earliest African Americans to write music for film. By the 1980s, Carter was considered a national treasure, touring around the world and winning many awards and honors.

The years covered in this chapter were the high point of the big band era. There were many bands, many different styles, many excellent soloists, and though the pop songs were not always memorable, the arrangers often used great imagination to create works of art. As we see in the next chapter, a confluence of events would lead to the beginning of the end of the big bands as the center of popular music.

5

THE WAR AND THE RECORDING BAN

1942–1946

The year 1942 was important both in world history and for big bands. The United States was now at war with Germany and Japan, so young Americans were being drafted and sent overseas. Within a matter of months, hundreds of excellent musicians were part of the war effort, many as part of military music ensembles sent across the United States, Europe, and the Pacific to boost troop morale. Ironically, two of the greatest bands in American music were created because of the war: Glenn Miller's Allied Expeditionary Forces (AEF) Ensemble and the Band of the U.S. Navy Liberation Forces.

As if that wasn't enough, music union president James Caesar Petrillo declared that recordings were negatively affecting opportunities for live performances, which meant less work for musicians. He wanted the record companies to pay royalties to the union to create a fund for live performances, threatening a ban on all recordings by union members (most of whom played in big bands). A report presented by industry veteran Ben Selvin stated that a recording ban would not create more live work and would hinder the activities of the musicians who were making records and generating money for the union. Petrillo disregarded this report and stated that from August 1, 1942, no union musician would record unless the record labels signed an agreement with the union and paid royalties. Decca and Capitol signed agreements in

1943, but Columbia and RCA Victor held out until late 1944. Few big band recordings were made during this two-year period.

In addition, gas rationing meant that ballroom attendance diminished, and bands couldn't travel large distances. An entertainment tax passed in 1944 affected any venue that served liquor and had a dance floor, further devastating the big band scene.

Thanks to radio, artists such as Frank Sinatra and Dinah Shore were now identified with the current hit songs. The bands kept going, but the going was tough!

When war was declared, Glenn Miller was adamant about joining the war effort. He disbanded in September 1942, volunteered for army service, and proceeded to put together one of the great popular music ensembles of all time. He handpicked the best of the draftees who played instruments to be assigned to his unit; string players came from leading American symphony orchestras. The ensemble had its own radio show for a year and made recordings for delayed broadcast. Eventually it was sent overseas to entertain the troops and made more recordings and broadcasts.

What: "In the Mood" by Joe Garland; arranged by Glenn Miller, Eddie Durham, and "Chummy" MacGregor
Where: CBS Playhouse No. 4, New York, NY
When: July 17, 1943

Recorded for an *"Uncle Sam Presents"* radio-only transcription, I am first struck by the sound quality of this recording. Miller's broadcasts benefitted from RCA's new high-fidelity equipment, and the power and drive of the ensemble are fully captured. Bassist "Trigger" Alpert had been with Miller's civilian band; drummer Ray McKinley was a veteran of many bands, including his own co-led with trombonist Will Bradley, and with the piano of composer and arranger Mel Powell from the Benny Goodman band, this rhythm section was one of the finest assembled for a big band during the swing era. Soloists are Vince Carbone and Jack Ferrier on tenor sax (1:02) and Bobby Nichols (who'd been lead trumpeter and soloist with the Vaughn Monroe Orchestra and would be a first-call musician in recording and television studios after the war) (1:28). Notice how the ending is repeated more times than the performance cited in the last chapter (when played live, this ending was repeated even more times), played softer and softer but still swinging hard. Also, listen to Ray McKinley providing "incidental talk," spurring the musicians on.

At one time, the only recordings of this ensemble easily available were issued on a five-LP boxed set by RCA Victor, which became difficult to get in later years. Happily, many more recordings have turned up and are in active circulation in excellent sound, including recordings made in England and France. Although this is a book about the jazz aspects of the big bands, I encourage you to listen to some of the band's ballads sung by the underrated Johnny Desmond.

As is well known, Miller lost his life traveling by plane from England to France on December 15, 1944. At this writing, there is still a Glenn Miller Orchestra touring and as busy as the one Miller himself led before the war. At one time, the Miller "ghost band" was led by jazz clarinetist Buddy DeFranco.

Artie Shaw joined the navy after breaking up his band in 1942. He led a group of musicians who toured the Pacific under harrowing conditions, and many of the men were severely affected by the bombing and shelling. Shaw obtained a medical discharge in 1943, and tenor saxophonist and arranger Sam Donahue became the new leader. Donahue was a veteran of the Gene Krupa Orchestra and led his own big band before he joined the navy. The new Band of the U.S. Navy Liberation Forces became one of the most exciting outfits of all time but was rarely if ever heard by the American public. In England, it participated in a "battle" of bands with Glenn Miller's AEF ensemble, and Miller called it the best of the service bands.

Happily, the band made several recordings for the armed forces called V-Discs, twelve-inch discs distributed to servicemen and women in the United States and overseas; the musicians donated their services because of the union ban. V-Discs were not distributed to the general public and were supposed to be destroyed after the war, but quite a few survive and are treasured by record collectors. The band also appeared on Armed Forces Radio.

What: "Convoy" by Sam Donahue
Where: CBS Playhouse Radio Studio, New York
When: June 12, 1945

Within a few seconds, the crisp brass and the powerhouse rhythm section show off the Jimmie Lunceford/Count Basie influences of this swinging ensemble. The piece is in AABA song form, the A melody played by six saxophones including Donahue, who also played trumpet and joined that section occasionally (0:10). In the B section, the piece changes key, and unison brass play the melody first, then in harmony (0:27). The A melody returns, and then Tak Takvorian solos on trombone (1:08). Donahue solos at 1:32. The A section returns with harmonized saxes and interspersed rhythmic figures by the brass (1:56), and then John Best solos on trumpet in the B section with unison sax backing (2:17). Rocky Collucio plays a piano solo (2:34), and Donahue returns (2:50). The entire band returns in the B section with saxes and brass calling and responding (3:11), and then the final A section is played with an exciting conclusion.

Donahue and the men wanted to stay together as an ensemble when the war ended, but the musicians were discharged at different times, and Donahue had to assemble a new group in 1946. He was signed to Capitol Records and made many excellent sides but never had the big hit he needed and was forced to disband in 1949. He led bands until his death in 1974, except for brief periods as a soloist with Woody Herman's band in 1958 and Stan Kenton's Orchestra in 1960.

Charlie Barnet was born into wealth, and became a bandleader at the age of eighteen. He had a popular band for several years, but in 1939, he had a huge hit record named "Cherokee," an instrumental written by bandleader Ray Noble and arranged by Billy May. Barnet's bands were always filled with good musicians, partly because the leader was a fun guy and the music was always great to play (Barnet was a great admirer of Duke Ellington, sitting in with the band once when one of the saxophonists was drunk).

Barnet's band gained even greater popularity during the war years and, most fortunately, had another solid hit in 1944, another anthem of the swing era.

What: "Skyliner" by Dale Bennett (aka Charlie Barnet); arranged by Billy Moore
Where: Decca Recording Studios, 5505 Melrose Avenue, Los Angeles
When: August 3, 1944

Written under the pseudonym of Dale Bennett to avoid paying alimony to several ex-wives, Barnet only wrote the saxophone melody, with former Jimmie Lunceford arranger Billy Moore writing the rest. Until the end of his life, Moore was bitter about being cheated out of a composing credit and the resulting royalties.

The track begins with a solo by a pianist who later worked with Artie Shaw and Boyd Raeburn, Michael "Dodo" Marmarosa. The brass play a melodic phrase that turns out to be counterpoint to the saxophone melody (0:11). Barnet plays soprano saxophone with the section, creating a full, rich sound; he was one of the few saxophonists who championed this instrument, as the horn was not easy to play in tune. Saxes take the first part of the B section of the melody (1:03), which is completed by a written solo by trumpeter Peanuts Holland (1:13). The A section is repeated, we hear a transition to another key (1:35), and then trombones alternate with Barnet's tenor (1:44). Marmarosa gets another solo (2:22), and the record ends with a repeat of the melody, the counterpoint, and an unusual ending in half-time.

Barnet continued to lead excellent orchestras and was one of the leaders who played bebop later in the era. We'll meet up with him then.

Billy Eckstine had been Earl Hines's vocalist from 1939 to 1943 and was considered one of the top singers in American music. The year 1943 was a crucial year for the Hines Orchestra, as many of the musicians in the band were pioneers of the new jazz subsequently called bebop, among them Charlie Parker, Dizzy Gillespie, and Sarah Vaughan. Due to the recording ban, there are no commercial recordings of this important ensemble, and no broadcasts have turned up.

Eckstine subsequently formed his own band, taking some of Hines's musicians with him. The group became a breeding ground for new talent, and such legendary musicians as drummer Art Blakey, tenor saxophonist Dexter Gordon, and trumpeters Miles Davis and Fats Navarro played with the orchestra at one time or another. In addition to Eckstine, Sarah Vaughan sang and played piano occasionally.

What: "Air Mail Special" by Charlie Christian and Benny Goodman; arranged by Budd Johnson
Where: Jubilee Program (Armed Forces Radio Service), Los Angeles
When: February or March 1945

From the very first notes, this is a powerful performance at a blistering-ly fast tempo that's totally different from the original recordings made by the Benny Goodman Orchestra and Sextet. No subtlety here—this band roars throughout! Sustained brass against the melody as the saxes play a chorus (0:08). A transition is heard (0:36), and then a solo by young Fats Navarro rips through the air—listen to his amazing technique and the huge sound he gets in every register of the horn (0:42). Another transition and the tenor saxophone of Budd Johnson rings out (1:19); Johnson was perhaps the oldest musician on the stand (he'd given saxophone lessons to Ben Webster), but he was also one of the hippest, embracing and mastering the new music and mentoring younger musicians. He is followed by tenor saxophonist Gene Ammons (1:47). Trombones have the melody after the transition (2:24). Then the melody is paraphrased for another chorus until the powerful ending, with Blakey hitting the drums for a finish.

As good as the band was, it was not a financial success, and Eckstine reluctantly disbanded in 1947. He later signed with MGM Records and recorded some big hits, but a promised screen career was denied him. He was a popular show business personality for the rest of his life, but he never achieved the legendary stardom that he certainly deserved. He is still lauded as an artist and a fashion icon who broke many show business barriers affecting African Americans.

Stan Kenton played piano and arranged for bands on the West Coast but always wanted to lead his own unit. In 1940, he made some test recordings and landed a summer gig at the Rendezvous Ballroom in Balboa Beach, California, in 1941. From the start, his band was either loved or hated by listeners and music critics. Those who loved the band thought it was exciting and modern; those who hated it thought it was too loud and didn't swing. Kenton's was one of the first bands signed to Capitol Records and could record anything the leader wanted. He was his own best promoter and later filled concert halls playing advanced music that he called "progressive jazz." He appears throughout the remainder of this book, and we start with one of his biggest hits with one of his best singers.

What: "And Her Tears Flowed Like Wine" by Joe Greene, Charles Lawrence, and Stan Kenton; arranged by Buddy Baker
Where: C. P. McGregor Studios, 729 S. Western Avenue, Hollywood
When: May 20, 1944

Vocalist Anita O'Day had been a star with the Gene Krupa band, and her name value helped the new Kenton band attract more attention. Two different takes of this recording exist, and they are a study in contrasts: the version issued originally is a fairly straightforward reading by O'Day, the second sounding far more improvised. Both are excellent and both YouTube links are cited at the end of this book.

The sharp, accented offbeats of the early Kenton style are reminiscent of Jimmie Lunceford's Orchestra, a band Kenton greatly admired. But the big ensemble sound that became his trademark is already in evidence. Pay particular note to what happens when O'Day completes her vocal; the key changes and the band shows off its power, driven by drummer Jesse Price (2:38), whom O'Day brought into the band. He remained only a short time, picking up a lot of gigs on the West Coast.

Tommy Dorsey's band had a ten-piece string section during the war years, and Dorsey was at the peak of his popularity. Once the recording ban was over, he was back in the studio to make one of the classic anthems of the big band era.

What: "Opus No. 1" by Sy Oliver
Where: RCA Victor Studios, Los Angeles
When: November 14, 1944

After a short introduction, a simple riff is the basis for this swinging classic, and it is the melody for all of the A sections of the AABA song form (0:03). The B section is particularly interesting, as it sounds like the piece is changing key but eventually returns to the original (very clever of Sy Oliver to do this) (0:25). For the second chorus, trumpets play a paraphrase of the melody (0:59), which leads to a clarinet solo by a young Buddy DeFranco; Dorsey would insist that DeFranco repeat this solo every time the piece was played, which DeFranco resisted (1:22). A piano solo by Milt Golden leads to a key change while the melody is paraphrased once again (1:45). DeFranco returns and ends his solo by leading the entire sax section in a virtuosic turn of phrase (2:09). The melody returns and an exciting ending is set up by Buddy Rich's drums; Rich has been swinging this large ensemble with rock-steady rhythm and powerful fills from the first note, and strings play a lovely background throughout (very often strings tend to slow the tempo down, but not here).

Many bands would cover this tune, and lyrics were later added by Sid Garis. The Mills Brothers and Anita O'Day featured this song in their acts over the years. It became one of Dorsey's biggest requests on the road, long after he dropped the string section.

Count Basie continued to lead his swinging band throughout the war, and the ensemble became a magnet for fabulous soloists and arrangers. Trumpeter Buck Clayton contributed many scores, as well as Buster Harding, who was also writing for Cab Calloway.

In 1945, a young trombone player and arranger joined the band who would later become a jazz giant. His name was J. J. Johnson.

What: "Rambo" by J. J. Johnson
Where: Liederkranz Hall, 111 East 58th Street, New York City
When: February 4, 1946

This was unreleased at the time, possibly due to an error in the trombone section at the beginning, but this track is now considered a classic,
and with lyrics added, it later became a feature for the vocal group
Manhattan Transfer.

Following an introduction, the AABA statement of the melody is
played by the band with trombones featured (0:09). The saxophone
section has a beautiful soli section (0:50) followed by Johnson's solo,
which already reveals a distinctive solo style (1:10). Illinois Jacquet solos
on tenor saxophone (1:28); he'd already established himself with a classic solo on Lionel Hampton's "Flying Home," and it was a great coup
for Basie to get him. A Basie solo (2:16) leads to a key change, with the
band playing a variant of the melody (2:27), followed by a trumpet solo
by Joe Newman (2:47), one of the standout soloists in Basie's 1950s
ensemble. A repeat of the A section of the melody (2:58) leads to an
exciting ending by the original Basie drummer, Jo Jones.

Duke Ellington was always in a class by himself. He continued to write
songs that became pop hits, and from 1945 to 1946, he had a weekly
one-hour radio show sponsored by the U.S. Treasury to advertise war
bonds; all of these shows have been restored and are available.

Billy Strayhorn continued to write arrangements for pop songs and
more ambitious compositions.

What: "Overture to a Jam Session" by Billy Strayhorn
Where: WOR Studios (Longacre Theater), 220 West 48th
Street, New York
When: December 11, 1946

A clarinet flourish by Jimmy Hamilton leads to the bass walking (the
legendary Oscar Pettiford, who would lead his own orchestra in the
1950s) (0:03). Brass instruments come in, leading to reeds (0:16). The
melody is played by harmonized saxes (0:55), with the B section played
by trumpet (1:21). After a statement of the last A of the melody (1:34), a

variation of it is played by saxes first (1:59) and then band. The ensemble plays held chords, and then an entirely new section is heard with
solo statements by violinist Ray Nance (2:57). Another variation of the
melody leads to the ending of the piece.

This composition took up two sides of a 78-rpm record and was part
of a new series of recordings made for a small label named Musicraft,
whose other artists included Artie Shaw, Georgie Auld, and Dizzy Gillespie. Unfortunately, the label did not last long in the marketplace and
was a memory by 1947.

Artie Shaw was in poor mental and physical shape when he was discharged from the navy. Rest and therapy helped him to get back into
music, and he soon fronted another spectacular big band. He was able
to get another superior soloist, trumpeter Roy Eldridge, who'd played
with Gene Krupa's band before the war. Once again, Shaw ran into
problems touring with a band featuring a black musician, and Eldridge
later left to form his own group but not before making some classic
recordings.

What: "Summertime" by DuBose Heyward and George Gershwin; arranged by Eddie Sauter
Where: RCA Victor Studios, Los Angeles
When: April 17, 1945

This is quite simply a masterpiece: a highly unusual, haunting treatment
of the Gershwin song that was already a standard, which was helped by
a major revival of *Porgy and Bess* in 1942. This recording is also another
example of an arrangement that could not be cut and had to be issued
on a twelve-inch platter. Reportedly, RCA Victor was not happy about
this and didn't want to release it. Shaw responded by leaving the label a
few months after this recording was made.

A tremolo in the bass clarinet leads into a sinuous bass line and sax
background (0:08) as Shaw plays the melody for a full chorus, one of his
loveliest solos on record (0:14). A tremolo in the piano and the background now in the trombones leads to an emotional, intense cup-muted
solo by Eldridge (1:24). After a mysterious-sounding transition that also
serves as a key change (2:19), the saxes switch to clarinet and play a

paraphrase of the melody with brass background (2:36). This paraphrase is eerie sounding and a great example of the musicianship in this ensemble, as the clarinets are in the highest part of their register and perfectly in tune. Tenor saxophonist Herbie Steward elaborates on the melody with an assist by Eldridge (3:03). Just as eerie is a piano solo by Michael "Dodo" Marmarosa either all alone or with harmonized clarinets (3:32), which is then followed by Shaw taking a partially unaccompanied solo (4:02). The ending is highly dissonant with clarinet and saxes holding a single pitch while the brass harmony shifts under it (4:30). The recording ends quietly with a piano flourish.

Shaw would disband in November and lead other ensembles, even playing and recording classical music for a time, but he would be back with another amazing band in 1949.

Woody Herman led an ensemble called the Band That Plays the Blues, but it was an all-around solid dance band; Herman had been a vaudevillian earlier in life and was a good clarinetist/alto saxophonist. In 1943, Herman hired bassist Chubby Jackson, who recommended several musicians he'd worked with in the Charlie Barnet band. Herman wanted to update his style, and by 1944 the band was playing a louder, more aggressive style of swing music with the arrangements of pianist Ralph Burns and trumpeter Neal Hefti. A steady engagement on a radio show sponsored by Old Gold cigarettes provided time and a national audience to further refine the band's new direction, and a new contract with Columbia Records in 1945 further signaled a new beginning. By 1946, Herman was leading one of the top bands in the country, with several excellent soloists.

What: "Happiness Is a Thing Called Joe" by E. Y. Harburg and Harold Arlen; arranged by Ralph Burns
Where: RCA Victor Studios, 145 East 24th Street, New York
When: September 5, 1944

A verbal introduction by vocalist Frances Wayne introduces this V-Disc heard by military personnel. Piano opens the track with Wayne singing a full chorus. The beauty of V-Discs is that these records were pressed on twelve-inch vinyl; the sound quality is excellent, and the perfor-

mance longer than the pop records being made at the time. Herman
has a solo in between Wayne's vocal (2:23).

What: "Sidewalks of Cuba" by Mitchell Parish, Irving Mills, and Ben Oakland; arranged by Ralph Burns
Where: Columbia Recording Studios, Los Angeles
When: September 17, 1946

When the band recorded this, Herman was leading a true all-star band;
the trumpet section included such outstanding musicians as Conrad
Gozzo and Pete Candoli (legendary soloists and first-call session musicians on the West Coast during the 1950s), trombonist Bill Harris,
guitarist Chuck Wayne, pianist Jimmy Rowles, vibraharpist Red Norvo,
saxophonists Flip Phillips, John LaPorta, and Mickey Folus (who'd
been in the Artie Shaw band), and drummer Don Lamond. Trumpeter
Milton "Shorty" Rogers became an important soloist and composer in
the 1950s.

Burns opens up this arrangement with a loud figure played by the
entire band; the A section is played by saxes (0:04). Herman solos on
clarinet during the B section (0:26) and brass and saxes alternate the
melody on the last A section (0:37). A wild, "Flight of the Bumblebee"
figure is heard (0:49), the beginning of a legendary solo by an extraordinary musician named Saul "Sonny" Berman. The solo showcases his
spectacular, Harry James–like huge sound and his technical fluency.
Wayne continues on guitar (1:16). An abrupt key change brings Herman back (1:38), then brass and saxes paraphrase the melody (2:00).
The beginning of the record is repeated (2:23) as the band gets softer
and softer, finally ending on a very soft chord with a drum hit to end
this incredible sound display.

When this recording was made, Berman was twenty-one years old
and attracting a lot of attention in the jazz world, but he died of a drug
overdose one evening at a party. His is another story of might-have-
beens, which are discussed throughout this book. As for the Herman
band, Woody disbanded at the height of the ensemble's popularity to
spend more time with his family, but he would be back with a new band
in 1947.

Ray McKinley was a drummer who co-led a band with trombonist Will Bradley; the ensemble was known for its boogie-woogie big band style. But Bradley was unsatisfied playing this music continually and the partnership was dissolved. McKinley assembled an excellent band of young musicians in 1942, but he was soon drafted and entered the army. Glenn Miller recruited him for his AEF Orchestra, and McKinley's playing was one of the highlights of this magnificent ensemble. When Miller died, McKinley became the leader.

Once out of the army, agent Willard Alexander suggested that McKinley start a new band with Eddie Sauter as chief arranger; Sauter wrote innovative scores for Red Norvo and Benny Goodman before the war. The idea was to balance modern composition with pop hits. The result was a unique ensemble that featured McKinley as drummer and vocalist with Sauter's instrumentals. The music was demanding, but once the band mastered Sauter's unique scores, it became one of the notable ensembles of the era.

What: "Hangover Square" by Eddie Sauter
Where: New York
When: July 9, 1946

With "Hangover Square," we experience one of the shifts in big band music. Though danceable, the form of this composition is different from what we've heard before and it sounds abstract. Repeated listening helps us determine how logical Sauter is in introducing and elaborating on his musical materials. Accented offbeats open this recording. In fact, the first part of the record doesn't even have a melody; it's mostly based on variations on the offbeat phrase heard from the very beginning. A repeated note on the piano brings us the second part (1:10), which does have a lovely melody in the saxes, repeated with trumpets playing offbeats (1:24). The B section of this part is played by trombonist Vern Friley (1:36), and when the A section is repeated, the trumpet of Nick Travis is heard (both of these statements are written in the music itself) (1:48). A transition brings us back to the beginning (2:04), which features the guitar of Mundell Lowe (2:15). Eventually the piece ends with a totally different musical phrase played and repeated by the entire band (2:57).

McKinley managed to balance the innovative with the popular until about 1949, when most leaders were finding it harder and harder keeping their ensembles working. He would later lead the Glenn Miller "ghost band" (a term used when the original leader of the band is no longer alive) for many years.

Buddy Rich was a child prodigy with his own drumming act in vaudeville who became a jazz drummer in small groups when he reached maturity. He joined the Artie Shaw band and was playing with Tommy Dorsey by the early 1940s. Cocky, contentious, and egotistical, he is acknowledged as one of the greatest drummers in the history of music. It was inevitable that he would start his own orchestra in 1946; one of his backers was Frank Sinatra.

What: "Dateless Brown" by Ed Finckel
Where: New York
When: February 5, 1946

Finckel had written for the Boyd Raeburn and Gene Krupa orchestras, and his type of exciting swing pieces fit the vision of Rich's band perfectly. Rich said he did not want to play anything slow, that even ballads would have a beat.

After a short introduction, the AABA song form begins with saxes playing both A sections (0:09), brass playing the B (0:27), and the saxes repeating the A. Trumpeter Bitsy Mullens plays a roaring solo (0:47), and George Berg solos on tenor sax (1:06). A key change brings a trombone solo by Earl Swope (1:25), saxes playing the B section (1:53), and a piano solo by Tony Nichols (2:02). Another key change (2:11) brings Mullens back. Rich solos (2:31) and after the band returns (2:40), the key changes again with a new strain (2:52), which ends the piece.

Rich lasted as a bandleader until 1948 and then toured with Jazz at the Philharmonic. He played with Harry James for several years, but he would be back as a big band leader in 1966.

Dizzy Gillespie was extending the language of jazz as early as his tenure with the Teddy Hill band in 1939, and along with fellow musicians such as Charlie Parker, Thelonious Monk, and Kenny Clarke, he helped to forge a new style of improvised music that came to be known as bop or bebop, a term the musicians despised. Originally a small-group music, Gillespie wanted to bring this new music to the big band format and led his first large ensemble in 1945 for a touring review called "Hepsations of 1945." The tour was a disaster, and Gillespie returned to New York but organized another edition of the band in 1946. This time he was successful, and the band made its first recordings in June.

What: "Our Delight" by Tadd Dameron
Where: New York
When: June 10, 1946

Dameron originally wrote this for the Billy Eckstine band, and when Gillespie needed music, Eckstine told him to go to his office and pick whatever he wanted.

After an introduction, the AABA melody is played by saxophones (0:16) and the B section is played by trombones and then the full band (0:38). After the last A, Gillespie solos with band background (1:00), the band plays the B section, and then tenor saxophonist Ray Abrams solos (1:27). The band alternates between Gillespie's solos (1:42) and the full ensemble ends the piece.

What: "One Bass Hit" by Ray Brown, Gil Fuller, and Dizzy Gillespie; arranged by Gil Fuller
Where: New York
When: mid 1947

"One Bass Hit" was originally recorded by Gillespie's sextet on May 15. The big band recording was issued as the "B" side, with the sextet version as side one, which is why this title is sometimes listed as "One Bass Hit, Part II."

What is presented here is a performance that was filmed for an all-black feature entitled *Jivin' in Bebop*. Ray Brown is the featured bassist, and since we can see the band in action, no description is necessary, except that it is Gillespie who plays the trumpet solo. The pianist is a young John Lewis, who later formed the Modern Jazz Quartet.

Boyd Raeburn had been the leader of a corny territory band that operated out of the Midwest. In 1943, he dramatically changed direction and came to lead one of the most adventurous ensembles in popular music. Dizzy Gillespie wrote "A Night in Tunisia" for the band, a tune that has become a jazz standard. Other musicians who were part of the ensemble at one time or another include arranger and future Academy Award–winner Johnny Mandel, pianist Dodo Marmarosa, trumpeter Ray Linn, trombonist Britt Woodman, and saxophonists Harry Klee, Hal McKusick, and Lucky Thompson. These fine musicians could have made a lot more money playing with other bands, but they chose to stay with Raeburn to play the swinging music by Ed Finckel, Milt Kleeb, Johnny Mandel, and especially the challenging scores written by composer/arranger George Handy.

What: "Dalvatore Sally" by George Handy
Where: Radio Recorders, 7000 Santa Monica Boulevard, Los Angeles
When: February 5, 1946

"Dalvatore Sally" was a play on the name Salvador Dali, an abstract artist. Resident in the United States since 1940, his influence permeated all of the art forms. This was the band's theme during this period, and it immediately identified the Raeburn Band as an avant-garde ensemble, although it was an excellent dance band and featured wonderful singers such as David Allyn and Ginny Powell.

"Dalvatore Sally" is so abstract that a description of it would be useless; the piece goes in and out of tempo and features no solos; it is truly a concert piece. It highlights an ever-growing movement to feature more abstract music scored for big band that would culminate in Stan Kenton's progressive jazz movement. There are more Handy arrangements that should be heard that showcase the breadth of his talent, and here is another one.

What: "There's No You" by Tom Adair and Hal Hopper;
arranged by George Handy
Where: Blue Room of the Palace Hotel, San Francisco
When: August 7, 1945

A very strange beginning reminds us of a fast, ethnic dance, followed by a dissonant piano solo. More dissonance in the full ensemble is followed by a calmer, warmer sound followed by David Allyn's vocal (0:31). During the second A section, the ensemble is clearly heard playing Debussy's "Clair de Lune" (0:56). A particularly lyrical section is the final A, where the accompaniment sounds like the woodwind section of a symphony orchestra (1:46). A key change brings the full ensemble playing the melody, with a clarinet solo by Hal McKusick (2:11). The vocal returns, and in the last A section there is a sly, abrupt key change (3:30). The recording ends softly, and most listeners would have to admit that they heard something unique in American music: a concert version of a pop song that is danceable.

Understandably, Raeburn never achieved any real financial success, although Duke Ellington and Harry James gave him money to continue. Even though Raeburn had to disband, he later led a larger orchestra with arrangements by Johnny Richards in 1947.

Despite the various restrictions on travel and entertainment, the war years were a time of tremendous musical growth in the big band world—larger ensembles and new sounds were starting to emerge that would inspire musicians and audiences yet alienate many listeners and dancers.

6

THE SINGERS TAKE OVER THE POPULAR
MUSIC SCENE

1947–1949

The men and women returning from the service wanted to buy homes and raise families, so fewer big bands were touring by 1947, and by 1948, people had another excuse to stay home—television. Yet this period resulted in some of the most interesting and beautifully swinging music up to that period. With the pop music scene dominated by singers, big bands experimented a bit, and new styles of music were heard. As we will see, bebop flourished in small groups and big bands, and bop combined with Latin sounds was called "cubop."

But first, we must discuss an ensemble that was first heard during the early war years that blossomed into one of the truly outstanding ensembles in American music after the war.

Claude Thornhill was a pianist who became known as the musical director of a recording sung by Maxine Sullivan on August 6, 1937, a jazzed-up version of the folk song "Loch Lomond." With Glenn Miller's encouragement, Thornhill formed his own orchestra in 1940, an ensemble that featured vibrato-less clarinets and brass backing his elaborate piano stylings. It featured beautiful, mellow ballads and swinging instrumentals featuring wide dynamic ranges from very loud to very soft, thrilling listeners and dancers. In 1941, he added French horns that made the orchestra sound even mellower. His chief arranger grew up on the West

Coast and once led his own band, which later became the nucleus of an ensemble led by singer Skinnay Ennis. This was none other than Gil Evans, who took Thornhill's basic ensemble approach and developed it further. Thornhill's band was moderately successful but broke up when Thornhill joined the navy.

After the war, Thornhill and Evans reassembled the orchestra, and Evans took this ensemble to incredible musical heights. The band played soft ballads that sounded like the type of dance music heard at hotel ballrooms and then jumping, exciting harmonically advanced be-bop-tinged instrumentals played by the more adventurous small bands of the day. I described this ensemble elsewhere as an avant-garde society band in that it delighted dancers with its slow danceable music yet thrilled listeners who loved hip modern jazz.

What: "Robbins' Nest" by Bob Russell, Illinois Jacquet, and Sir Charles Thompson; arranged by Gil Evans
Where: Associated Transcriptions Studio, New York
When: October 16, 1947

Although Thornhill recorded this for Columbia Records the following day, this radio-only recording features the complete arrangement, and I believe the performance is superior.

Beginning with a piano introduction, the introduction continues with instrumental colors that are mixtures of saxophones and brass that are blended so skillfully that we often cannot tell which instruments are playing together, part of the uniqueness of Evans's style. Although Evans still features groups of instruments against each other, they are not simply saxes versus brass, but trumpets versus French horns, trombones, and tuba. Thornhill plays the melody in both A sections, separated by a brief statement by saxes, trombones, and tuba (0:13). The B section is played by clarinet, saxophones, and French horns, a warm, rich color (0:46). Cup-muted trumpets play the last A section (1:02), leading to a solo by clarinetist Danny Polo (1:18). During the second part of his solo, listen to the saxophone line against brass punctuations and how the ensemble becomes loud and then quickly soft at the end of the solo (1:34). Polo and tenor saxophonist Mickey Folus trade off on the melody (1:50).

What happens next is one of the most striking instances of melodic paraphrasing during the late big band era. The entire ensemble plays a harmonized, improvisational-sounding line that sounds like one big instrument, perfectly balanced and relaxed. Again note the dynamic range from very soft to very loud (2:05). Thornhill returns for the last part of the B section (2:30), and then the ensemble plays the A section again in unison (2:38). The ensemble introduction returns (2:52), ending with a quiet dissonant chord resolving into a rich, consonant chord as Thornhill plays piano fills and the piece ends.

What: "Yardbird Suite (What Price Love)" by Charlie Parker; arranged by Gil Evans
Where: Liederkranz Hall, 111 East 58th Street, New York
When: December 17, 1947

This is an excellent example of a bebop instrumental composition adapted for dance band.

There were various places in the beginning of the arrangement that were cut or not recorded, perhaps because the arrangement needed to fit on a ten-inch record (many of the arrangements discussed are available to play and study, and they are complete). In this recording, piano plays the two A sections of the song with a slight interruption by the band (0:09). There is a sudden key change (0:22), and the full band plays the two A sections with the saxophones playing the B (0:45). Lee Konitz contributes an unusual solo on alto saxophone (1:08) followed by trumpeter Red Rodney (1:36). Another key change introduces the guitar of Barry Galbraith (2:00). The piece ends in a very strange way: initially the melody is heard, and then Evans begins a paraphrase that turns dissonant (2:56) until a final chord, followed by a drum finish.

There are other equally amazing Thornhill recordings from this era that are readily available. Several were arranged by Evans, but he also brought in such arrangers as Gerry Mulligan and John Carisi to add to the Thornhill book. Eventually Thornhill wanted to go back to his original vision of the piano being the main soloist for ballads and dancing and Evans left. But the Thornhill Orchestra remains one of the key ensembles in orchestrated modern jazz of the 1940s and would be the model for the Miles Davis nonet. Thornhill had a band on and off until his death, and we revisit this ensemble in chapter 7.

Dizzy Gillespie's orchestra continued presenting unadulterated bebop to its many audiences, and a 1948 European tour proved a major success despite poor management. The music both stunned and upset jazz listeners; some musicians later described how this new musical direction fired them up, yet more traditional jazz fans were disturbed and sometimes reacted violently. There were fights and some longtime friendships ended.

Many European audiences also had their first experiences with Latin music during the Gillespie band's concerts. When he started the orchestra, Gillespie was interested in incorporating Cuban music in his orchestra's repertoire and asked former Cab Calloway trumpeter Mario Bauza for advice. Bauza recommended percussionist and composer Chano Pozo, an acquaintance from Cuba. Pozo spoke no English but managed to make himself understood to Gillespie nonetheless. Although the styles of modern jazz and Latin music were very different (jazz being swing based and Latin more rhythmically even), the musicians in Gillespie's orchestra soon adapted. Pozo also could not read or write music, but he heard the entire orchestra in his head, and one day sang a melody and accompaniment to Dizzy, outlining what instruments should play what musical lines. Gillespie called arranger Gil Fuller to write everything down as Pozo sang it, harmonizing and organizing the piece so that it could be played. Fuller soon had score and parts ready.

What: "Manteca," composed by Chano Pozo; adapted and arranged by Gil Fuller
Where: RCA Victor Studios, 155 East 24th Street, New York
When: December 30, 1947

This track was recorded right before a second recording ban in 1948 over royalties paid to the music union by the record labels.

Beginning with a bass pattern, another pattern is set up in the saxes (0:09). Gillespie solos as the band builds (0:20), an explosion of chords is heard (0:31), and the famous A melody is played, started by saxophones and answered by the brass (0:39). The B section is in another key, played by saxes (1:01), then Gillespie (1:12), and then the A section is played again (1:24). A transition leads to the band swinging with a tenor saxophone solo by George "Big Nick" Nicholas playing on the two A sections (1:49). The B section begins with full band and then Gillespie solos again (2:22). The band goes back to Latin rhythms as the A section returns (2:34). The piece becomes softer and softer until Pozo and the drums finish it off.

Pozo led a very colorful life and had a volatile personality; he was murdered in a Harlem bar in December 1948. He was replaced, but a steady decline in bookings was affecting big bands as the decade ended, and Gillespie wound up playing novelties before disbanding in 1950 (one of his saxophonists was a young John Coltrane). He led important ensembles in later years, and we discuss one of his finest ensembles a bit later.

Woody Herman's new band was called the Second Herd, because the earlier (1944–1946) unit was referred to as the Herman Herd in the trade press. He found a group of new musicians who played bebop, and the group was characterized by the makeup of the saxophone section, which included one alto, three tenors, and a baritone sax; this became known as the "Four Brothers" sound.

What: "The Goof and I" by Al Cohn
Where: Columbia Studios, Los Angeles
When: December 27, 1947

Tenor saxophonist Al Cohn originally wrote this for the Buddy Rich orchestra. Cohn was one of many Herman sidemen who would become stars in their own right.

Herman leads off with band background and then the melody is heard in the saxes (0:16). The B section features call and response between the brass and unison saxophones (0:37), then the brass take over the melody. A transition (0:57) leads to the baritone saxophone of Serge Chaloff, an excellent soloist who would die much too young in 1957. Another transition brings us to the trombone solo of Earl Swope

(1:45) and then to a Herman solo (2:06). A key change (2:26) brings the entire band in to finish the recording.

What: "Early Autumn" by Johnny Mercer and Ralph Burns; arranged by Ralph Burns
Where: Capitol Records, 5515 Melrose Avenue, Los Angeles
When: December 30, 1948

On March 25, 1946, the Herman band played a successful concert at Carnegie Hall, featuring two new compositions: "Ebony Concerto" by none other than Igor Stravinsky and a suite of three pieces by Ralph Burns entitled "Summer Sequence." When the Herman band came to record "Summer Sequence," a fourth piece was added to fill out two single discs, which were later issued in an album. By the time the fourth piece was recorded for Capitol, the melody was adapted as a popular song with lyrics added by Johnny Mercer.

The recording opens with the classic "Four Brothers" sound of three tenor saxophones and one baritone sax. Herman solos on alto (0:57), and Terry Gibbs solos on the last A section (1:27). A key change then leads to the improvisational lyricism of a young Stan Getz (2:06), who had already played with Stan Kenton and Benny Goodman. This solo became so well-known that Getz became a star and soon left to lead his own groups.

After playing with Louis Armstrong and Benny Goodman, vibraphonist Lionel Hampton formed his own band in 1941 and had a huge hit with tenor saxophonist Illinois Jacquet, "Flying Home." This was one of the most exciting bands of any era, but Hampton also explored more modern sounds in the late 1940s.

What: "Mingus Fingers" by Charles Mingus
Where: Decca Recording Studios, 5505 Melrose Avenue, Los Angeles
When: November 10, 1947

Mingus was attracting a lot of attention on the West Coast when he joined Hampton, who played several arrangements Mingus wrote, including an excellent arrangement of "Body and Soul." This is Mingus's show, showing his deft technique and huge sound (even his bowing is excellent, not surprising since Mingus began as a cellist) (1:00). Even today, this composition sounds unusual, and it is to Hampton's credit that it was recorded. Decca Records was still a rather conservative label in 1947, but since there was a recording ban in 1948, I guess they took a chance.

Hampton led a band for many years; since his was one of the first to record rhythm and blues ("Rag Mop," "Turkey Hop"), he was popular at rock and roll shows during the 1950s. He died in 2002.

In 1946, Count Basie's mentor, John Hammond, encouraged him to sign with a new label called Majestic. Instead, Basie's manager made a deal with RCA Victor, which turned out to be a poor decision based on some of the material Basie was "asked" to record (however, to be fair, Majestic Records was out of business by 1947). Once thought to be the worst recordings Basie made, quite a few of the RCA Victor sides are excellent and worth hearing.

What: "Normania" ("Blee Blop Blues") by A. K. Salim
Where: RCA Victor Studios, 145 East 24th Street, New York
When: August 5, 1949

On or slightly before the time of this recording, Basie decided to break up the band, but he left a souvenir of what would be one of the mainstays of his new band of the 1950s, often called the "New Testament" band. "Blee Blop Blues" would later be played at an outrageously fast tempo (tenor saxophonist Frank Foster told me that there was no way any performance could be played without some mistakes), so it is a treat to hear it as it was originally envisioned.

Basie starts on piano followed by a trumpet solo by Harry "Sweets" Edison (0:16). This piece is a blues with the melody stated (0:33), leading to a tenor saxophone solo by Bill "Weasel" Parker (0:55). Next is one of the earliest solos by trumpeter Clark Terry, one of the most beloved instrumentalists in the history of jazz who was a member of the Ellington orchestra for many years and then a studio player who later led his own big band (1:21). A transition (1:40) leads to a saxophone section solo (2:03). The band plays two choruses, and then the piece ends with a short saxophone statement.

Basie would lead an all-star interracial octet in 1950 that left some excellent recordings, but he jumped at the chance to reassemble another large ensemble, and by 1951, he was back in the big band business.

Benny Goodman led a fascinating small group in 1948 that included the tenor saxophonist Wardell Gray. This ensemble was clearly bebop influenced, although Goodman said he didn't care for the music. Later that year, he formed a big band that featured Gray and several other young players who had absorbed the new harmonic and rhythmic sounds. Like Charlie Barnet and Gene Krupa, Goodman tried leading a modern jazz orchestra, even playing updated versions of his biggest hits.

What: "Undercurrent Blues" by Arturo (Chico) O'Farrill
Where: Hollywood Palladium, Hollywood
When: March 29, 1949

The U.S. Government continued transcribing broadcasts of popular music for servicemen and women overseas after the war, and this performance comes from a "One Night Stand" program of live music. Arturo O'Farrill was chief arranger for this ensemble, although Billy Byers, Gerry Mulligan, and Johnny Mandel contributed music as well. "Undercurrent Blues" had been recorded a month earlier at Capitol Studios, but this live broadcast allows us to hear the entire piece.

The melody is played by the full band (0:13), trombonist Milt Bernhart solos (0:45), then Gray solos (1:16). (Gray's solo was cut for time on the commercial recording.) A brief orchestral statement introduces trumpeter Doug Mettome's solo (1:46). A change of key brings a solo by

Goodman, clearly still playing in his classic style and not incorporating any of the new rhythms or harmonies (2:30). The full band plays a paraphrase (3:05) and a short piano statement by Buddy Greco (3:22) brings back the melody in a different key (3:28). The band ends the piece with a powerful chord.

This ensemble was as good as any Goodman ever led, but he was uncomfortable with the new music and didn't treat the musicians very well (this would not be the last time that a Goodman ensemble would have poor morale because of Benny's behavior). Gray was later murdered in Las Vegas under mysterious circumstances.

Gerald Wilson was first known as the trumpet player and arranger who replaced Sy Oliver in Jimmie Lunceford's band. Wilson served in the navy, and in 1945 he was asked by vocalist Herb Jeffries to put together a band to accompany him. A tour was arranged, but Jeffries backed out at the last minute, and Wilson decided to keep the band going. Wilson's ensemble was very successful, one of the first to play bebop (his recording of "Groovin' High" was produced months before Dizzy Gillespie's big band played it), toured all over the country, and even accompanied singer Dinah Washington at Mercury Records, where he'd signed a contract. But he decided things were happening too fast and disbanded so he could study music formally, a decision he always thought was a wise one. Almost immediately, he got a call from Duke Ellington to play in his band and write arrangements. In 1947, he assembled a studio-only band for some recordings.

What: "Dissonance in Blues" by Gerald Wilson
Where: Los Angeles
When: late 1947

Now considered an influential recording because of its unusual way of presenting a minor blues, essentially this is a feature for bassist Red Callender (who also played excellent tuba). At the very beginning, saxophones play highly dissonant chords that move to rhythmic punctuations as Callender solos (0:11). Saxes play sustained chords as Callender continues (0:47), and then there are two choruses in which the full band plays. For the first chorus, saxes have the melody with brass "comments" (1:21); part of chorus two plays in double time (the music sounds twice as fast but is in the same tempo) (2:05). Throughout we are struck by how different the harmony is; this isn't a standard blues as played by Count Basie. Callender plays his next solo with the bow (2:30), finishing the recording.

Wilson later wrote and toured with Count Basie in 1949 and led bands in the coming years. We return to him when we examine the big band scene in the 1960s.

While attending Duke University, Les Brown led a band on campus. He later turned professional, arranging for various bands as well as leading a unit of his own. One day a young girl named Doris Day joined as the group's singer, and both band and singer began attracting a lot of attention. Day left to marry and have a son but returned after she divorced her husband, making many wonderful recordings and later signing a contract with Warner Bros. Pictures. By that time, Brown's band was the musical ensemble for Bob Hope's radio series and later became identified with Hope on television and various USO ours for servicemen and women. It is only within the past few years that the Brown ensemble has been recognized as one of the top ensembles in American music, and it was his contract with Hope that allowed Brown to continue to commission excellent music and have important jazz soloists.

What: "I've Got My Love to Keep Me Warm," by Irving Berlin; arranged by Skip Martin
Where: Columbia Recording Studios, Los Angeles
When: September 16, 1946

Skip Martin wrote quite a few excellent arrangements for the Brown band and the vocal group the Pied Pipers; he was also an arranger/orchestrator for M-G-M motion pictures in the 1950s and transitioned to television in the 1960s.

Why is this recording here instead of in the previous chapter? Columbia Records didn't release it when it was first recorded, perhaps because it was written by Irving Berlin in 1937 for a musical film called *On the Avenue* and was not a current pop hit. In 1948, the arrangement was played on Bob Hope's radio show and got great audience reaction. According to Brown, he received a wire from Columbia to come in and record it. Brown wired back saying, "Look in your vault." Columbia released the record, and it became one of Brown's biggest hits.

Although this is a straightforward rendition of the tune with solos by tenor saxophonist Ted Nash (0:59), pianist Geoff Clarkson (1:36), and trumpeter Jimmy Zito (2:00), what probably made this a hit is the light, bouncing, danceable tempo. As late as 1949, big bands were still making recordings that became big hits and would continue to do so in the coming years. Although there were fewer bands on the road after 1950, touring big bands were still a viable part of show business. "I've Got My Love to Keep Me Warm" reportedly sold more than a million copies and was recorded many times by the Brown ensemble.

Francisco Raul Gutierrez Grillo was born in Cuba. Called "Macho" by his parents, his name later became Machito. He became a professional percussionist and played in many ensembles in Cuba, later coming to the United States in 1937. At that time, ensembles playing Cuban music were made up of strings and a woodwind or two. Machito wanted to form an ensemble with a larger brass section like the swing bands. He formed an ensemble with his friend Mario Bauza and made some recordings in 1941. Machito was drafted in 1943 but soon returned after a leg injury. Bauza sent for vocalist Graciela from Cuba, who was Machito's foster sister. Machito and the Afro-Cubans became a sensation after the war, and pianist George Shearing and leader Stan Kenton were only two of many musicians greatly influenced by this new music, which featured the Cuban style with congas and bongos fused with jazz improvisation. Machito even played maracas in Kenton's band for the recording of "The Peanut Vendor," one of Kenton's biggest hits, and the two bands split a concert at New York's Town Hall. Machito had several guest soloists for recordings and live gigs who played in the new style of bebop, and the word *cubop* was coined to describe the music. Machito played Latin dances as well as jazz clubs and even made some films.

What: "Tanga" by Mario Bauza
Where: New York
When: January 1949

"Tanga" had been Machito's theme since 1943. This recording illustrates how the Machito ensemble played the fusion of Cuban music and jazz.

This recording features what is called a "montuno," a repetitive riff-like figure represented by one chord throughout. "Tanga" does not have a theme, simply a collection of riffs that build and then recede. At the very beginning, the riff starts in the piano, percussion comes in with saxophones playing a sustained background as Machito sings (0:14). The full band plays a transition (0:59) and then alto saxophonist Gene Johnson solos as the background builds (2:11). A rhythmic figure in the saxes begins as guest tenor saxophone soloist Flip Phillips begins a solo as riffs go in and out, all backed by the percussion section (3:18). The record ends abruptly with Phillips finishing his solo.

Along with the Tito Puente and Tito Rodriguez bands, Machito played regularly at the biggest Latin dance ballroom in New York, the Palladium. We visit Machito and Puente a bit later.

Stan Kenton acquired an arranger/composer who'd obtained his master's degree in music studying composition with the distinguished concert composer Darius Milhaud. Pete Rugolo began writing unusual arrangements of popular songs, but Kenton encouraged him to write whatever he wanted. The resulting original music was often challenging to listen to, but was also stimulating and often groundbreaking. Kenton wanted to turn his ensemble into a concert unit and began to book his orchestra into concert halls while continuing to play dances. It helped that Kenton was an excellent salesman for his music, and concerts were sellouts all over the country. This edition of Kenton's ensemble became known for playing "progressive jazz." It was one of the few times in American music where modern music reached a wide audience as well as the interest of concert composers (Leonard Bernstein was a big fan of the Kenton ensemble).

Some of Kenton's most popular recordings were Latin- and Cuban-based compositions and arrangements.

What: "Machito" by Pete Rugolo
Where: Radio Recorders, 7000 Santa Monica Blvd., Los Angeles
When: March 31, 1947

This was the second studio recording of "Machito;" an earlier version was recorded on February 13.

Four big chords begin this piece, and then the melody is played by Kenton's piano (0:05). Kai Winding, a major influence on the way the Kenton trombone section played, is next heard playing the melody (0:30). A transition by the entire band leads to a key change (0:56), with Chico Alvarez playing the melody as the band plays more and more intensely (1:09). The ten-piece brass section comes out roaring as they play the harmonized melody (1:33) followed by a trumpet/trombone duet played by Buddy Childers and Skip Layton (whose high register is remarkable even today) (2:04). This section is still challenging to play, and both musicians worked on it to make it sound as good as it does here.

This is a classic example of the three- to four-minute concert pieces that the Kenton band played at the time. Many were even issued in study score format, a first for big bands, in which arranger/composers could study the music in detail.

Kenton continued to sell out ballrooms and concert halls but was exhausted by the punishing touring schedule and disbanded in December 1948. He contemplated becoming a psychologist, but music was his calling, and he would be back in 1950 with one of his biggest orchestral adventures.

Duke Ellington played his first Carnegie Hall concert in 1943, and premiered a large suite entitled "Black, Brown and Beige." Reviews were mixed, and it was said that Ellington was so disturbed by the reception of his music that he rarely composed anything so ambitious again. He gave several concerts at the prestigious concert landmark throughout the 1940s and always had new concert music to play. In 1947, Ellington was commissioned by the government of Liberia to write a composition for that country's centennial. Ellington responded with the "Liberian Suite." Made up of an introductory song and five dances, it was Ellington's second LP, issued in 1948. The suite was premiered at Carnegie Hall on December 27, 1947.

What: "I Like the Sunrise" by Duke Ellington
Where: Liederkrantz Hall, 111 East 58th Street, New York
When: December 24, 1947

After a long introduction, Al Hibbler sings a full chorus of the song, a performance that singer and arranger Mel Torme later called, "one of the gentlest, most moving vocals ever put on wax." Baritone saxophonist Harry Carney also has an extensive solo (2:34). This was an early example of overdubbing, in which the vocal was recorded at a different time than the Ellington ensemble. This would become common when recording tape became widely used in 1948, replacing recording directly on an acetate disc.

We first met Chubby Jackson when he was playing bass for Charlie Barnet and Woody Herman. He left to form various small groups and took one of them to Europe, where it recorded in Sweden. He formed a big band in early 1949, and although it was made up of fourteen men and a vocalist, it sounded much bigger than it was thanks to drummer Norman "Tiny" Kahn's arrangements and compositions.

What: "Father Knickerbopper" by Norman "Tiny" Kahn
Where: The Royal Roost, 1580 Broadway, New York
When: March 5, 1949

A blisteringly fast tempo is established by the rhythm section on this live recording. Brass play introductory figures interspersed with rhythm fills as Jackson screams. The melody is in the saxes in unison (0:35); it's amazing that this tricky passage sounds so organized and together. We are fortunate to hear Kahn's drums so clearly; notice his heavy offbeats on the bass drum to drive the band. The piece is in AABA form, and after the last A, Teddy Charles solos on vibes with brass punctuations (1:01). Marty Flax has a brief solo on baritone sax (1:52) followed by Al Young (2:00). Frank Socolow (who'd played with Boyd Raeburn) plays a short solo on alto sax (which was not his regular horn) (2:06), and then a long solo is played by Ray Turner, an excellent young player who was a

Jackson discovery (2:12). Al Porcino solos for the rest of the track with band backing (2:32) until the band plays a short melodic phrase leading to a powerful final chord. The result is breathtaking, an exciting piece that is over almost as soon as the track has begun.

The Jackson band didn't last long; Chubby sounds like a maniac on some of the airchecks that have been preserved, and its powerful bebop sound was not what most audiences wanted to hear. But this band left some stunning performances, and its influence would be felt around the world. Tiny Kahn would go on to play drums and write excellent arrangements for the Elliot Lawrence band (his friend, composer/arranger Johnny Mandel, told me that he considered Kahn one of the most talented musicians he knew; Mandel would later play with Count Basie and won Academy and Grammy awards). But Kahn had a weight problem and died of a heart attack at the age of thirty.

Ted Heath was one of Britain's top trombonists playing in Ambrose's and Geraldo's bands and appearing in jazz sessions, most notably with Benny Carter. Heath befriended Glenn Miller when the American AEF (Allied Expeditionary Forces) ensemble was broadcasting in London, and Miller encouraged him to form his own unit. Heath's first BBC broadcasts were made up of musicians from various bands; however, the BBC's new rule that only full-time, professional bands could broadcast forced him to give up his chair with Geraldo and create a permanent band of his own. Originally a "sweet" ensemble, Heath's band became one of the greatest swing and jazz ensembles of all time, with excellent arrangers and soloists.

Due to strict rules imposed by both the British and American musicians' unions during the Depression, Heath's band was not heard live by American audiences until 1956. The first time American listeners got to hear the Heath band was in 1948 via a three-record album of Fats Waller music on London Records (which was the American agent for British Decca). Listeners were captivated by the Heath band's beautiful, huge sound and its powerful swing. In 1949, Heath began incorporating bebop music into his repertoire.

What: "Father Knickerbopper" by Norman "Tiny" Kahn
Where: Decca Studio No. 2, London
When: September 1949

Kahn wrote a stock arrangement of his tune (as described in chapter 1, stock arrangements were versions of songs and compositions that were printed and marketed for any bandleader to buy and play); except for the piece being in an entirely different key, the arrangement is almost exactly the same. Somebody on the Heath arranging staff wrote additional parts so that the seventeen-piece band could play the piece.

We hear that the tempo is a bit slower than the original Chubby Jackson recording, but this music is still challenging and the Heath band sounds well-rehearsed. Soloists are Dave Simpson on piano (0:49), Dave Shand on baritone sax (0:57), Henry McKenzie on tenor sax (1:05), Les Gilbert on alto sax (1:13), Tommy Whittle on tenor sax (1:22), and Ronnie Hughes on trumpet (1:47). Hughes seems to be the most conversant with the new harmonic language of bebop and is clearly influenced by Miles Davis.

Heath's was always a disciplined unit, and although some may feel that the ensemble is a bit stiff, it is still a swinging machine. The lack of sonic clarity on the recording is attributed to the small studio in which it was recorded; historians have always wondered why the Heath band was recorded in studio 2 rather than the larger and more resonant studio 1. In later years it would be back in studio 1, where it would make its greatest recordings.

By 1949, Charlie Barnet led a remarkable band that played bop and Cuban music. Barnet hated most of this music and disbanded after a few months, but these recordings have gained in stature among big band historians, and one allows us to experience one of the great composer/arrangers of that era, Paul Villepigue.

What: "Lonely Street" by Paul Villepigue
Where: Capitol Records Studio, 5515 Melrose Avenue, Los Angeles
When: January 16, 1949

Paul Villepigue was born in Kansas in 1919 and played with local bands but eventually made Chicago his home base, writing for the Boyd Raeburn and Chico Marx orchestras (yes, *that* Chico Marx of the Marx Brothers). Villepigue was in the military from 1943 to 1946 teaching music, and upon discharge, went to New York. Johnny Bothwell was the alto sax soloist for Boyd Raeburn, and when he formed his own orchestra, Villepigue became chief arranger. Villepigue later wrote for Harry James and Stan Kenton and for singers such as Mel Torme; he also taught at Westlake College of Music in Los Angeles. Tragically, he committed suicide in 1953.

"Lonely Street" is perhaps Villepigue's most well-known of his compositions and arrangements. Soprano saxophonist Barnet plays the melody in both A sections, supported by clarinets and cup-muted trumpets in the first A. Full band supports Barnet for the second A (0:30), and the B section melody is played by the solo trombone of Dick Kenney (0:59). The melody continues in the unison trumpets with trombone chords under it and the saxes playing a counter line (note the richness of the saxes here; there are six saxes instead of five) (1:28). The B section is repeated with soprano sax (2:02), and then the last A is played as in the beginning (2:31). A short ending by brass finishes the piece.

Judging by his music, Villepigue admired the Duke Ellington Orchestra. This piece reminds us of Billy Strayhorn's "Chelsea Bridge" based on its harmony and the mixed orchestral color of clarinets and muted trumpets. Other work by Villepigue shows an original talent who was widely admired by the musicians who played and sang his arrangements.

In 1948, Columbia Records introduced the long-playing (LP) disc. Ten-inch LPs were initially the size for pop and jazz albums, and the earliest LPs were compilations of previously released recordings; the ten-inch disc was phased out in 1957. The sound was much improved, and the discs themselves more durable. Although several ensembles like Duke Ellington's stayed on the road, many of the great big bands were studio-only groups assembled for particular recording projects. Now that the big band ceased to be the center of popular music, the opportunities for more ambitious music grew. The last chapters of this book chronicle some of the most notable music for large jazz ensembles and great soloists.

7

REBIRTH AND DIVERSITY

1950–1959

At the beginning of the decade, some big bands continued to play ballrooms, hotels, and colleges, but as far as pop music, singers had the majority of the hits; the fare was mostly novelty songs such as "How Much Is That Doggie in the Window?" and "If I Knew You Were Coming, I'd've Baked a Cake." At the same time, black radio stations were playing a new style of music called rhythm and blues, a style that would develop into rock and roll. "Rock around the Clock" was not a hit when it was first released, but when it became part of the soundtrack for the movie *The Blackboard Jungle*, it was rereleased and took off. And then one day on the TV program *Stage Show*, hosted by bandleaders Tommy and Jimmy Dorsey, a young kid named Elvis Presley appeared on national television. Rock and roll and doo-wop groups dominated popular music during the latter half of the 1950s.

The big band was flourishing in the recording studios and on television shows; some musicians worked from 7:00 am till 2:00 am, and there was plenty of work to go around. Some studio-only ensembles became so popular on records that they went out on the road.

We've already met both Eddie Sauter and Bill Finegan in these pages—Sauter as arranger for Red Norvo, Benny Goodman, and Ray McKinley, Finegan for Glenn Miller and Tommy Dorsey. Sauter and Finegan were close friends, and Sauter wrote to Finegan one day about a bandleader who rejected one of his arrangements. To make his friend feel better, Finegan told Sauter that perhaps they should start their own ensemble. Eddie took him seriously and agreed, thus was born one of the most beloved and innovative ensembles ever formed in American music.

The Sauter-Finegan (S-F) ensemble was perfect for the times. As stated earlier, the popular music scene was filled with novelty songs, and the S-F band recorded its share of novelties. Its very first record, "Doodletown Fifers" was an adaptation of a Civil War song called "Kingdom Come and the Year of Jubilo," and it featured all sorts of woodwinds and percussion. At times the S-F band, as it came to be called, sounded more like a concert ensemble than a big band, and that was part of its appeal. It recorded songs that were popular sellers ("Nina Never Knew" with a vocal by Joe Mooney is considered a classic) as well as standards. The pop records provided the freedom for Sauter and Finegan to write concert pieces.

What: "Solo for Joe" by Eddie Sauter
Where: Webster Hall, 125 East 11th Street, New York
When: November 2, 1954

From an album called *Concert Jazz*, this is an original composition by Sauter featuring the improvisation by Joe Venuto on marimba, the background either consisting of (1) a glee-club effect of the musicians singing or playing the melody behind the soloist (if you listen closely, you can hear trumpet and tenor sax playing as part of the glee-club effect) (0:14) or (2) Venuto continuing his solo backed by guitar, bass, drums, and celeste (2:17). The effect is haunting and almost surreal. But the S-F band was known for unusual directions in the presentation of original compositions and standards, with striking instrumental solo and ensemble colors, vocal groups, harp, and a wide array of percussion. It was not unusual to hear oboe and English horn, harmonica, a kazoo ensemble, and even a toy trumpet on S-F recordings. The music was so creative and so artfully done that these did not come off as gimmicks.

Although it wasn't meant to be a road band, Eddie and Bill were pressured to turn the band into a touring ensemble for several years until bookings dried up, and it disbanded in 1957. The ensemble recorded two more albums for RCA Victor, but by that time Sauter was in

Germany leading the Sudwestfunk radio ensemble while Finegan free-lanced in New York. When Sauter returned in 1959, they recorded two additional albums and worked on various projects together.

The S-F band remains one of the most unique ensembles in American music and has been cited in arranging books for its profound influence on composer/arrangers. Every professional arranger I've spoken to has S-F records, and it was a badge of honor to be part of the ensemble when they recorded (Elden C. "Buster" Bailey, percussionist with the New York Philharmonic, said that recording with Sauter and Finegan was the most fun he had in the music world, other than playing in a circus band). It also had an effect on instrumentalists: by the mid-1950s, saxophonists were expected to play not only saxophone and clari-net, but flute as well, if they wanted the choice recording and television jobs then proliferating in New York and Los Angeles.

While Les Brown's Band of Renown remained the musical ensemble backing Bob Hope's television and live appearances after World War II, it continued to play numerous dance gigs on the West Coast. It was always stocked with excellent musicians and soloists; many remained with him for years, as Brown was a great leader to work for and the music was always of high quality. In September 1953, the band played an extended engagement at the prestigious Hollywood Palladium Ball-room, and a two-LP set of its performances was released by Coral Records. Multirecord sets were rare for pop and jazz artists in those days; however, it was fortunate that his label went to the expense of preparing and releasing the album, as the results show that this was one of Brown's finest bands.

What: "Montoona Clipper" by Wes Hensel
Where: Hollywood Palladium, 6215 Sunset Blvd., Los Angeles
When: September 1953

Composed by trumpeter/composer Wes Hensel, this is a feature for tenor saxophonist/bass clarinetist Dave Pell, who'd been with the band for several years by the time of these Palladium performances. The band originally recorded the piece in the studio in November 1952, but the electricity of a live crowd makes this performance more exciting.

The introduction is especially interesting: musical layers are added one by one, first by bass instruments with Latin rhythm accompaniment, a layer by two trombones (0:04), another layer by more trombones (0:07), a layer by saxes and trumpets (0:14), and then Pell has a tenor solo break before the rhythm section continues (0:22). The melody is in AABA song format, with saxes in unison playing both A sections with brass punctuations (0:29), the B section played by harmonized brass with sax fills (0:43). Then the A is repeated, the "layer additions" of the intro are played (0:56), and then Pell goes into an extended solo on one chord with musicians in the band adding various Latin percussion as they shout encouragement (1:20). After a transition, the AABA song form repeats as the piece ends.

Brown balanced jazz with danceable music until his death in 2001. At this writing, his son Les Brown Jr. has kept the band going in Branson, Missouri. Pell would form an octet that featured a book of arrangements that allowed him to play dances at colleges as well as gigs at jazz clubs, and his ensemble made many excellent recordings. Pell became a producer of recordings as well. He passed away in 2017.

As discussed in the last chapter, Claude Thornhill continued to lead a band on and off until his death in 1965. In 1953, he recorded an album featuring an arrangement that Gerry Mulligan wrote for him in 1949.

What: "Jeru" by Gerry Mulligan
Where: New York
When: April 28, 1953

In 1949, Mulligan was one of the chief participants in the organization of the Miles Davis Nonet. Originally a rehearsal band, the ensemble played a handful of gigs and made some records. Mulligan originally composed "Jeru" for Davis and also wrote a version for Thornhill. What we notice is the clarinet lead at the beginning when the melody is played by saxophones (in fact, the Davis Nonet was to have clarinetist Danny Polo in the ensemble, but he passed away; alto saxophonist Lee Konitz replaced him). The bridge shifts time from 4 to 6 to 3 (0:22) before returning to 4 for the end of the B section and a solo by tenor saxophonist Ray Norman (0:31); the A repeats with an extension. Trumpeter Dick Sherman plays a solo (0:51) and Norman returns (1:13). The ensemble plays in 3 (1:35) as Norman continues when the time returns to 4. The ensemble continues as clarinetist Med Flory solos (2:36) and the ensemble ends playing chords off the beat (2:51) until the held chord at the end.

This arrangement was cut for time; most fortunately the original manuscript exists and was edited by me for publication.

Johnny Hodges, Lawrence Brown, and Sonny Greer left Duke Ellington to form their own group, but all except Greer would return a few years later. In the interim, Ellington continued playing concerts and dances and wrote more pieces that became standards.

What: "Satin Doll" by Johnny Mercer, Duke Ellington, and Billy Strayhorn
Where: Capitol Studios, 5515 Melrose Avenue, Los Angeles
When: April 6, 1953

Not an immediate hit when it was first recorded, Ellington played it constantly until the piece became established. After Ellington's piano intro, the ensemble enters and tenor saxophonist Paul Gonsalves has a short solo (0:48). There's a brief trumpet solo by Ray Nance playing the B part of the song (1:36) before the ensemble plays a variation of the melody (1:58). The melody returns (2:20) and Ellington has the last word on the piano.

Billy May played trumpet and arranged for Charlie Barnet and Glenn Miller. Eventually he became a freelance arranger for radio, television, and recordings. By 1950, he was arranging music for pop and jazz singers and composing scores for children's recordings at Capitol Records. He wrote arrangements for an album of dance music based on the Jimmie Lunceford two-beat style of the thirties, featuring "slurping" saxes (saxes sliding up to a given pitch). The Capitol executives were so impressed that the recordings were issued as singles, and "All of Me" became a big hit. Follow-up recordings were so popular that May took a band on the road, but he was ill-suited as a public front man and sold the band to Ray Anthony. He arranged and conducted for Nat "King"

Cole, Frank Sinatra, and other big stars while continuing to make top-selling albums.

What: "The Sheik of Araby" by Harry B. Smith, Francis Wheeler, and Ted Snyder; arranged by Billy May
Where: Capitol Studios, 5515 Melrose Avenue, Los Angeles
When: November 15, 1955

May's album "Sorta Dixie" is a tour-de-force satire of early jazz written and performed with great affection. Several of these arrangements were later adapted for the Boston Pops when John Williams was the musical director.

For this album, May's orchestra was made up of his standard brass sections, with French horn and tuba, woodwinds, rhythm, and percussion added. But the ensemble also included a Dixieland front line consisting of trumpet (Dick Cathcart), trombone (Moe Schneider), clarinet (Matty Matlock), tenor sax (Eddie Miller), banjo/guitar, piano, bass, and drums.

"The Sheik of Araby" is a great example of a popular song written in response to a local or world event. In this case, it was written in 1921 based on the popularity of the motion picture, *The Sheik*, one of the films that made heartthrob Rudolph Valentino a star. "The Sheik of Araby" became a standard that has been performed and recorded many times by such artists as Louis Armstrong and even the Muppets.

May's version of this classic song may be the most unique of the bunch. It begins with an English horn playing a sinister-sounding Middle Eastern musical line with interspersed "comments" by percussion (love the gong!) and the Dixieland front line (0:17). A quote from Saint-Saens's opera *Samson and Delilah* is blasted by the brass and timpani (0:50), then the front line plays the song, interrupted by the big band; listen to the "slurping" saxes and the xylophone in the background (1:00). A brass transition leads to the full band playing the verse of the song (1:36), with the clarinet and lead trumpet showing off in their high registers (Conrad Gozzo plays trumpet here, a reminder that he was one of the top lead trumpeters in California at that time) (1:48). Note how part of the bridge is played by piccolo, English horn, and French horn with harp background (2:13). Short statements by the Dixieland group lead to a colorful transition with a solo by the English horn, one of the rare improvised English horn solos in the history of jazz and big bands (Julie Jacobs is the soloist) (2:28). After this, the Dixieland group returns for a bit (3:10).

Then May throws us another curve: another melody from *Samson and Delilah* is played by full brass (3:30), finally leading to a restatement of the "Sheik" melody (with some great piano fills by Paul Smith) (3:49), the return of the Dixie group (4:17), a restatement of the *Samson and Delilah* melody at the top of the arrangement (4:24), more of the sinister solo English horn (4:31), and then a slam-bang ending.

May cited this as one of his favorite albums of his own work and wrote that it cost a lot of money to make but became so popular that it became profitable many times over. When he made public appearances overseas in the 1980s, titles from this album were always requested and enthusiastically received.

Shorty Rogers was born Milton Rajonsky and played trumpet and arranged music for a Red Norvo small group in 1943. By 1946, he was playing and arranging for the Woody Herman Orchestra and worked with Stan Kenton in the early 1950s. He became one of the key figures in a style of music called West Coast jazz; his music was often subtle and sometimes experimental during the decade under discussion (he was a composition student of Dr. Wesley LaViolette). An RCA Victor recording contract resulted in many albums with his "Giants," which could be a big band or a small group. Although he led small groups in public more often than not, he also made some live appearances with a big band (recordings of one or two of these are in circulation).

Rogers figures in an early use of jazz and Latin music for dramatic purposes in a motion picture.

What: "Hot Blood" ("The Wild One") by Leith Stevens; arranged by Shorty Rogers
Where: RCA Victor Studios, Los Angeles
When: July 14, 1953

In 1951, the music for *A Streetcar Named Desire* was hailed as a major breakthrough for jazz as the basis for a motion picture background score. It was written by Alex North, who wrote other jazz-tinged scores for film as well as ballet and concert music. "The Wild One" had another groundbreaking background score utilizing jazz. The music was written by veteran radio and film music composer Leith Stevens, and Rogers orchestrated the big band sections.

The Wild One was originally to be called *Hot Blood*, hence the title of the track. Marlon Brando starred as the leader of a biker group that caused a violent incident in a small town; this film reinforced Brando's image as a cool, mysterious antihero. Controversial upon release, the film was banned for fourteen years in the United Kingdom.

Rogers recorded four selections from the movie for an extended-play (EP) release, a record that played at 45 rpm and had two cuts per side. This was a popular format for a few years but was phased out in the United States by the late 1950s. (European record labels continued to release EPs into the 1960s.) Besides trumpets, trombones, saxes, and rhythm, the ensemble includes a French horn and tuba.

The sound of a motorcycle revving up begins and ends the track. This is high-powered, strong music with brass roaring and upward swoops from the French horn. Shelly Manne's drums hammer out a figure that sounds like bullets from a machine gun (0:15). The track alternates between a Latin-type beat and then swing as the track progresses (0:57). This is truly an all-star ensemble: trumpeters Maynard Ferguson, Conrad Gozzo, and Ray Linn were all high-note specialists as well as soloists of note. John Graas's French horn is a standout. The saxophone section included world-class soloists such as Bud Shank, Herb Geller, Bob Cooper, Jimmy Giuffre, Bill Perkins, and Bill Holman. Trombones were Harry Betts, Bob Enevoldsen, and Jimmy Knepper. Practically every musician in this band was also a talented composer/arranger. I list the musicians on this track to illustrate that it was now possible to hire an ensemble for any type of record on either coast in which every musician was among the best in the country, and most of them got their starts in road bands.

In 1954, Rogers made an album as a tribute to the 1930s and 1940s Count Basie band.

What: "Topsy" by Edgar Battle and Eddie Durham; arranged by Shorty Rogers
Where: RCA Victor Studios, Los Angeles
When: February 2, 1954

After an introduction, tenor and baritone saxophones play the A part of the melody (0:14), the B played by the full band (0:41). Rogers solos with a straight mute (1:08), and Herb Geller plays a solo on alto saxophone (1:36). The full band plays until a solo by tenor saxophonist Jimmy Giuffre (2:19). Marty Paich plays a piano solo (2:32) and then the melody returns in the saxophones (2:46). The introduction is repeated until a held chord at the end.

In addition to his excellent albums with the Giants throughout the 1950s, Rogers arranged for singers as part of his RCA contract; he also suggested that Henry Mancini record his music for the television show *Peter Gunn*, a landmark album and one of many Mancini recorded for the label. By the 1960s, Rogers stopped playing to concentrate on writing music for film and television but picked up the horn again in 1982 to make recordings and tour. He died in 1994.

One of the most gifted and talented musicians to lead a big band, Tito Puente grew up in Spanish Harlem in New York City. Mastering the piano and the saxophone, his true passion was percussion, whether it was timbales or vibraphone. He played percussion in Machito's Orchestra until he was drafted in 1942, and after serving in the navy, he attended the Juilliard School of Music and studied theory, composition, and orchestration. He formed his first band in 1948, and from the beginning blended Latin music with jazz, often arranging the music himself and writing original compositions. The Palladium Ballroom in New York City was the hotspot for Latin bands, and Machito, Tito Puente, and Tito Rodriguez were regularly featured there. Hollywood stars regularly came to dance and listen, and dancing lessons were available for those who were new to the exciting new dance, the mambo.

For years, Puente recorded for the Tico label, but by the mid-1950s, he was an RCA Victor artist.

What: "Live a Little" by A. K. Salim
Where: Webster Hall, 125 East 11th Street, New York
When: March 8, 1957

Stereophonic sound was first introduced in motion pictures in 1952 via the three-paneled Cinerama process, and films made in the widescreen process CinemaScope included a four-track stereophonic soundtrack (though many theater owners didn't invest money in the sound systems of their theaters, and many movie patrons heard the sound in mono). By 1957, quite a few record labels were recording in stereo and issuing the results on open-reel tape; it wasn't until mid-1958 that the stereo LP was perfected and marketed. RCA Victor began recording concert music in stereo in 1953, but pop and jazz were not recorded stereophonically until 1956.

The sound of "Live a Little" is spectacular, and the music perfectly illustrates a musical setting with drums playing swing, but congas and bongos playing Cuban rhythms; even though they are different, they blend together beautifully. Marty Holmes plays a tenor sax solo (he also wrote for the Puente band) (0:46), and guest Carl "Doc" Severinsen also solos on trumpet (he would later become the bandleader on *The Tonight Show Starring Johnny Carson*) (1:30).

Puente made several influential albums during this period but soon left RCA Victor to return to Tico.

Along with touring and residencies at the Palladium Ballroom, Machito's band continued to make excellent recordings during this era as well. Alto saxophonist Cannonball Adderley and flautist Herbie Mann were guests when Machito made albums for the new Roulette label.

What: "Cannonology" by A. K. Salim
Where: Metropolitan Studios, New York
When: December 24, 1957

Originally a school music teacher in Florida, Cannonball Adderley was first heard in New York at the Café Bohemia when Oscar Pettiford's saxophonist didn't show up for a gig and Cannonball was asked to sit in for the night. It wasn't long before word got out that a "monster" musician was in town. Adderley reminded listeners of the recently deceased Charlie Parker with his excellent technique, harmonic mastery, and bluesy sound.

After an AABA statement of the melody, it is Cannonball for most of the track (0:37). A brief interlude of percussion instruments (1:37) leads to a repeat of the AABA melody with a brief tag.

When Adderley made this recording with Machito, he was a member of the Miles Davis ensemble and ended the decade leading his own group with his brother Nat. He would lead this group for the rest of his life.

What: "Blues a la Machito" by A. K. Salim
Where: Metropolitan Studios, New York
When: December 24, 1957

Another example of the blending of jazz and Latin music, this track begins as a series of fanfares. The melody is played by the saxophones with brass punctuations (0:10) and one feels that this would be just as effective without the percussion. Count Basie trumpeter Joe Newman is the chief soloist (0:59).

After his big band broke up in 1950, Dizzy Gillespie toured with small groups. But with Quincy Jones's help, he assembled a band in 1956 for a U.S. State Department–sponsored Middle Eastern tour; the band also toured South America. This was an excellent unit that included Phil Woods on alto sax, Melba Liston on trombone, and Charlie Persip on drums. Melba Liston, Ernie Wilkins, A. K. Salim, Quincy Jones, and Dizzy Gillespie created a new book of music, and before the band left, they recorded two LPs worth of old and new scores.

What: "Dizzy's Business" by Ernie Wilkins
Where: New York
When: June 6, 1956

From the very first loud chord, this is a powerful, swinging piece. An earlier version of this melody was written and recorded as "Cymbalisms" for an album called *Drum Suite* on March 7, 1956. "Dizzy's Business" is no longer a drum feature, just a straight-ahead AABA piece with solos, but with an interesting extended final A section before Gillespie's solo (0:59). The alto saxophone solo later in the track is played by Phil Woods (1:50). Wilkins also wrote a great amount of music for both the Count Basie and Tommy Dorsey bands during the 1950s, and musicians loved playing his music.

This exciting band stayed together after the tour and played several dates across the country, but once again, there just weren't enough gigs to keep the ensemble going, and it was a memory by 1958.

Count Basie was forced to break up his band in 1949 and led an all-star octet as the 1950s began, but it was inevitable that he would lead a big band again, assembling a new one in 1951 for a gig at the Apollo Theater. Called the New Testament band (his 1936–1950 group was considered the Old Testament), the sound of the band was updated by arrangements written by Neal Hefti, Ernie Wilkins, Frank Wess, Frank Foster, and Thad Jones but still maintained the relaxed swing that made it famous. By 1955, the Basie ensemble featured a roaring new sound and powerhouse collection of soloists: tenor saxophonists Wess and Foster, trumpeters Joe Newman and Thad Jones, and trombonists Henry Coker and Benny Powell. Freddie Green was back at the guitar chair, his relaxed yet powerful pulse joining bassist Eddie Jones, drummer Sonny Payne, and of course Basie with his distinctive, minimalist piano comments. The ensemble always played at Birdland when in New York and was identified with the club.

Basie had quite a number of hit recordings during this era, but one of the biggest was the result of the work of another keyboard player who happened to share the bill at Birdland when Basie was performing there.

What: "April in Paris" by E. Y. Harburg and Vernon Duke; arranged by William Strethen "Wild Bill" Davis
Where: Fine Recording Studios, 711 5th Avenue, New York
When: July 26, 1955

Davis was an arranger who began playing jazz on the electronic organ, and when he played his version of "April in Paris" at Birdland, Basie knew that it would be a strong addition to his book. Davis arranged it for the band and planned to record it with the Basie crew, but ultimately the ensemble recorded it without him.

After an introduction, the song is introduced by saxes (0:15). Henry Coker plays the bridge (0:44). Trumpet player Thad Jones begins his improvised solo with "Pop Goes the Weasel," which helped to make the arrangement a hit but also forced Jones to play it over and over, sometimes twice a night (1:15).

The other element that made the recording a hit was an exciting ending (2:02), after which Basie says, "one more time," and the band does indeed play the last minute or so of the arrangement once more (2:33). He then says, "let's try it one more once," and the same section is repeated one last time (3:09). After the recording became a hit and the band played it on the road, when the "one more once" section was played, the trumpets would play the melody of "Jingle Bells," no doubt something that the band came up with one night.

"April in Paris" helped to make this ensemble internationally popular among jazz and non-jazz listeners. It was a rare gig indeed if the song was left out, as audiences shouted out, "One more time!" and "One more once!"

Another important composer/arranger for Basie during this era was the tenor saxophonist Frank Foster.

What: "Blues in Frankie's Flat" by Frank Foster
Where: Unknown, probably European television
When: ca. 1958

This live performance features the entire composition before the piece was cut and renamed "Blues in Hoss' Flat" in honor of an American DJ. After the introduction, the trombones play the melody. After a muted trumpet solo by Joe Newman (0:37), Foster solos (1:15). The band plays a paraphrase of the melody (1:53) and Henry Coker solos (2:13). After a Basie solo, a softly played paraphrase is heard (3:13) and then played very loudly. The last statement roars (3:53) and then decreases in volume. Joe Newman has another solo before the piece ends.

Jerry Lewis later licensed the piece and the recording for a segment in his motion picture *The Errand Boy*, making this composition world famous.

Needless to say, seeing the Basie band during this period is priceless and too good not to feature more from this televised concert.

What: "Cute" by Neal Hefti
Where: Unknown, probably European television
When: ca. 1958

Hefti's compositions certainly became classic big band standards, and his pieces for Basie are still being played by school and professional bands around the world.

A Basie solo leads to the famous melody (0:52). Frank Wess plays a flute solo (1:25), leading to a drum solo by Sonny Payne (2:30). Saxophones have a written-out chorus before the band plays the melody again (3:01).

Stan Kenton began the 1950s with one of the great experiments in American music, the Innovations Orchestra. The full Kenton Orchestra of five saxophones, five trumpets, five trombones, piano, bass, and drums was joined by strings, French horns, and percussion. Three- to four-minute concert pieces were newly commissioned, and the ensemble played concerts throughout the country for two seasons. During the summer, Kenton played dance gigs to make up the sizeable amount of money he lost on the Innovations tours. Although the ensemble often sold out large halls, there were many concerts that took place in venues too small to turn a profit.

Kenton followed this up with another excellent band with music written by William Russo, Gerry Mulligan, Willis "Bill" Holman, and Johnny Richards. For a short time, Kenton featured Chris Connor, who had a big hit with the song "All about Ronnie" and went on to become an international star.

Kenton's bands didn't swing all out in the traditional sense like the Basie or Ellington bands, one of the key criticisms of Kenton's music, so critics and Kenton's many fans were surprised when in 1955, Kenton commissioned Bill Holman and Gerry Mulligan to write out-and-out swing material. As with all Kenton bands, this edition had some of the best musicians in the country: trumpeters Al Porcino, Sam Noto, and Stu Williamson, trombonists Bob Fitzpatrick and Carl Fontana, and saxophonists Charlie Mariano, Lennie Niehaus, and Bill Perkins. Perhaps the key element of this swinging outfit was the drumming of Mel Lewis, whose style was not the flashy, loud, pushing approach championed by such drummers as Buddy Rich or Art Blakey, but a subtle, gentle, supportive approach highlighted by unique cymbal work.

What: "Stompin' at the Savoy" by Andy Razaf, Edgar Sampson, Benny Goodman, and Chick Webb (although it is acknowledged that the main credits should be Razaf and Sampson); arranged by Bill Holman
Where: Universal Studios, Chicago
When: July 22, 1955

This is an early masterpiece by Bill Holman, who is celebrated as a composer whose music derives from musical lines entwining, intersecting, and often layering. Although much of his music is certainly written to be played by large ensembles, his work often sounds like it was written with a small group in mind and made up on the spot. Yet all of these new melodies Holman creates based on the original are restated and elaborated upon, turning his work into recomposition. "Stompin' at the Savoy" was an instant classic when it was released and has been published and performed by hundreds of bands the world over.

The melody is never stated as originally written but is paraphrased. After this first statement, cup-muted trumpets have a counter line (0:14). Open trumpets have the melody for the B section of the tune (0:30), and the paraphrase counter line returns, leading up to a guitar solo by Ralph Blaze (0:55). Additional solos are played by trumpeter Stu Williamson (1:53) and tenor saxophonist Bill Perkins (2:18). The ensemble at 3:20 is a paraphrase of the melody leading to the out-chorus (3:29). Listen to all of the melodies that Holman creates that are similar to the original and the other phrases that complement them. Listen also to how he combines them into something original by the end (4:07), creating a satisfying ending. It's no wonder that Holman's music is studied in composition classes.

In 1956, Kenton commissioned Johnny Richards to write the music for an album of "authentic" Latin music. "Cuban Fire" is now considered a classic of world music.

What: "Recuerdos (Reminiscences)" by Johnny Richards
Where: Riverside Plaza Hotel Studios, W. 73rd Street, New York
When: May 22, 1956

The Kenton Orchestra is joined by guest tenor saxophonist Lucky Thompson, who played with Boyd Raeburn and several other big bands and who went on to have a successful solo career in the United States and France. Note that the makeup of this edition of the Kenton orchestra is unusual: four saxophones (one alto, two tenors, one baritone), five trumpets, two French horns, four trombones, tuba, guitar, piano, bass, drums, timpani, and five of the top Cuban and Puerto Rican percussionists in New York.

The piece is a guajira, derived from a Cuban country or peasant dance. Percussion instruments include bongos, conga drum, guiro (a gourd with notches in it, creating a scratching sound when played with a drumstick), claves (thick wooden sticks), cowbell, and timbales (high-pitched drums).

Trumpets have the melody after the long introduction, with Thompson soloing on the tenor sax (0:43). The trombones and French horns play the B portion of the AABA song form (1:23), with Kenton playing solo piano on the last A (1:41). A transition leads to an alto solo by Lennie Niehaus (2:08). Sam Noto solos on trumpet (2:52) and Carl Fontana solos on trombone after a key change (3:45).

Along with Jimmie Blanton and Charles Mingus, Oscar Pettiford was one of the most influential bass players during the 1940s and had incredible technique on the cello as well. He was part of the Charlie

Barnet band in 1943 and then played bass with Duke Ellington's orchestra. He formed several small groups during the 1950s and made many recordings. But he always wanted to form a big band of his own, and the instrumentation was certainly unique: two trumpets, two French horns, trombone, four saxophones, harp, piano, bass, and drums.

What: "Smoke Signal" by Gigi Gryce
Where: New York
When: June 12, 1956

After an introduction by piano and harp, a fast tempo is established and the A melody is played (0:26). Saxes have the B section (0:52) and the A section returns. Alto saxophonist Gigi Gryce solos (1:18), drums and full band are featured before trumpeter Art Farmer solos (2:21). Tenor saxophonist Lucky Thompson (2:47) and trombonist Jimmy Cleveland solo (3:00) before Osie Johnson has a drum solo. He transitions to waltz time (3:35), and the band plays the melody in 3 before going back to the fast 4 tempo (3:45). The melody is repeated with more drum statements by Johnson before the track ends.

Pettiford became dissatisfied with work conditions in the United States and moved to Europe in 1958, dying of a rare virus in 1960.

Before Johnny Richards joined the Kenton orchestra as a composer/arranger, he was in Hollywood for most of the 1930s writing and orchestrating music for Paramount Pictures, as well as for top stars such as Eddie Cantor and Bing Crosby. In 1940, he led his own big band and played adventurous dance music until the ensemble disbanded in 1945. He later arranged for Boyd Raeburn and Harry James and wrote an album of arrangements for Dizzy Gillespie and concert orchestra. Richards contributed to the Kenton Innovations ensemble then wrote for the Kenton Orchestra from 1952 on. As stated earlier, Richards wrote "Cuban Fire," and the success of the album was immediate and worldwide, so much so that Kenton encouraged Richards to form his own band. In 1957, the Richards Orchestra played gigs in the New York and New Jersey area and signed a contract with Capitol Records. In 1959, the Richards ensemble made a final album for Coral Records, mixing

ambitious Richards originals with arrangements of standards for dancing.

What: "Walk Softly" by Blanca Webb and Johnny Richards; arranged by Richards
Where: Decca Studios, 50 West 57th Street, New York
When: May 14, 1959

Richards had written one standard called "Young at Heart," which
Frank Sinatra recorded and became a huge hit; "Young at Heart" became the Richards band's theme. Richards continued to write pop
songs, of which "Walk Softly" is particularly notable. While this is a
straightforward rendition of the song, it is interspersed with solos by
tenor saxophonist Frank Socolow (a veteran of the Raeburn and Jackson
orchestras) (0:18) and the muted trumpet of Burt Collins, a recording
session mainstay for many years (1:59).

The Richards Orchestra is yet another example of a large big band
with slightly different instrumentation from traditional big bands. Richards's reed section consists of alto sax, tenor sax, baritone sax (doubling
flute and piccolo), and bass sax, four trumpets, three trombones,
French horn, piano, timpani/percussion, bass, and drums. Piccolo and
French horn colorings are very prominent, making this ensemble sound
more symphonic than most jazz orchestras.

Ultimately Richards was forced to disband this ensemble and returned to write for Stan Kenton. The combination of these two powerhouse musicians would combine in another musical adventure discussed in the next chapter.

After he left the Claude Thornhill ensemble, Gil Evans wrote arrangements for the Miles Davis Nonet. This ensemble was designed as a
rehearsal band that sounded like the Claude Thornhill Ensemble, and
Evans influenced its design and instrumentation (he originally envisioned a clarinet instead of an alto saxophone, and there is a clarinet
part on one of his two arrangements, "Moondreams"). After 1950,
Evans seemed to have vanished from the jazz world.

He was hardly inactive. He wrote many of the arrangements for the
big band led by trumpeter Billy Butterfield, played piano for singers

and in clubs, and wrote for recording dates (Pearl Bailey, Al Martino, Gerry Mulligan, Tony Bennett). Columbia Records producer George Avakian asked him to contribute arrangements to Johnny Mathis's first album and reunited him with Miles Davis when the trumpeter was signed to the label. Evans and Davis were to make four albums at Columbia, the first being *Miles Ahead*.

What: "Springsville" by John Carisi; arranged by Gil Evans
Where: Columbia 30th Street Studio, New York
When: May 23, 1957 (trumpet solo overdub on May 27th)

The opening track to the first Davis/Evans collaboration at Columbia Records is like a rallying cry for a new sound and approach to the big band. The ensemble is made up of alto sax and three reed players doubling on flute, oboe, clarinet, and bass clarinet, five trumpets, four trombones, two French horns, tuba, bass, and drums; in essence, this was a brass band with woodwind colors. This album is unusual in that it is arranged as two long medleys (one per each LP side) with no stop in between songs, the same format that composer/arranger Michel Legrand used for such pop albums as "I Love Paris" and "Castles in Spain." This was the first time the full-LP-side-as-medley concept was used for a big band album.

After a short introduction by Davis, he plays the melody as the rhythm starts in a blisteringly fast tempo (0:04). Almost immediately the brass roar an answer (0:07). Davis and the brass trade phrases as the woodwinds add color (0:12). Davis solos with bass and drums with woodwinds and French horns commenting softly beneath (1:02). Suddenly bursting out, the entire ensemble plays figures based on the first part of the tune (1:59), only to have Miles reappear (2:16) and eventually recapitulate the track by repeating the beginning as the ensemble eventually winds down (2:59) with brass in mutes leading directly into the next piece.

Davis toured with various small groups and recorded music that is considered some of the most important jazz of the century. But *Miles Ahead* fully established Gil Evans as one of the most influential arrangers of all time. By 1959, he'd recorded three albums of his own, and all were considered important musical statements.

George Russell was a drummer who became a composer/arranger in the mid-1940s. He became fascinated with the theoretical side of music and designed a concept of music called the Lydian Chromatic Concept of Tonal Organization, which became an indirect influence on Miles Davis and his most famous album, *Kind of Blue*. Russell created new scales based on the Lydian mode and wrote a textbook first published in 1953.

Russell recorded an album based on the concept in 1956, and it received rave reviews. In 1958, he was signed to record a big band album, which had New York City as its central theme.

What: "Manhattan" by Lorenz Hart and Richard Rodgers; arranged by George Russell
Where: Decca Studios, 50 West 57th Street, New York
When: September 12, 1958

After a recitation by Jon Hendricks accompanied by drummer Charlie (later Charli) Persip (0:06), a long introduction ends with a bass note and drums (1:49). A steady tempo is established, and what takes place can probably best be described as an abstract musical design with the elements of the melody and harmony of the Rodgers–Hart standard. The melody is only stated occasionally in snippets, and the original harmonic sequence is not followed until the solo sections, which are essayed by trombonist Bob Brookmeyer (3:12), and then Brookmeyer alternating with trombonist Frank Rehak (4:13). Pianist Bill Evans solos next (5:03), one of his earliest solos; he would become one of the most influential musicians in jazz in just a few short years. Tenor saxophonist John Coltrane has a solo (7:10), and we hear him at a crucial time in his development when he was finding his direction, playing in the style that jazz writer Ira Gitler would later call "sheets of sound." Coltrane plays very rapid scale-like figures with a vibratoless, full tone that was a shock to many listeners, even though he'd made a few albums prior to this appearance. Reportedly he needed a lot of time to prepare for the solo, making several of the other musicians impatient. But the end result was stunning and certainly a highlight of the album, which had many. Art

Farmer has a trumpet solo before the track ends (9:27) with Coltrane soloing again.

Russell made several more albums with smaller groups in the 1960s. One of his commissions involved an ensemble that Gerry Mulligan organized in 1960, which is explored in the next chapter.

Johnny Dankworth was an alto saxophonist who was one of the first British musicians who mastered the bebop style. He arranged for Ted Heath, who wanted him to join his organization full time, but Dankworth put together the Johnny Dankworth Seven after meeting and jamming with Charlie Parker at the Paris Jazz Festival in 1949. By 1953, he formed a big band noted for its powerful swing, varied orchestral colors, excellent soloists, and the arrangements by Dankworth and Dave Lindup. In 1956, he created one of the great big band novelty recordings.

What: "Experiments with Mice" by Johnny Dankworth
Where: EMI Studios, London
When: May 10, 1956

Though not strictly a jazz record, this was a big hit for the Dankworth ensemble. With narration by Dankworth himself, this was a recording that used the song "Three Blind Mice" to satirize the big bands of Billy May (0:19), Benny Goodman (0:41), Glenn Miller (1:00), Gerry Mulligan (1:40), Sauter-Finegan (2:00), and Stan Kenton (2:26).

The Dankworth band had a slightly unusual instrumentation compared to most big bands during the late 1950s: five trumpets, five trombones, three reeds (including Dankworth), piano, bass, and drums.

The band played at the Newport Jazz Festival in 1959 and shared stages with Duke Ellington and Louis Armstrong. Dankworth maintained this ensemble and also became a composer for television and motion pictures.

When an album named *The Mystery Band* was released in the United States in 1957, listeners marveled at the sound and swing of the ensemble, convinced it was a new American band. Finally the secret was out: the mystery band was led by Swedish tenor saxophonist and arranger

Harry Arnold (Harry Arnold Persson), who'd been leading big bands since 1942. The band was so good that Quincy Jones wrote for it and directed the ensemble for broadcasts and recordings. At the time, Jones was studying composition with the distinguished pedagogue Nadia Boulanger, whose students included Aaron Copland, Robert Russell Bennett, and Michel Legrand.

What: "The Midnight Sun Will Never Set" by Dorcas Cochran, Henri Salvador, and Quincy Jones; arranged by Jones
Where: Stockholm, Sweden
When: April 29, 1958

This is an alto saxophone feature for Arne Domnerus, one of the leading jazz soloists in Sweden. In May of the same year, Sarah Vaughan recorded this with Quincy in Paris, France. When Quincy Jones led his own band (see next chapter), this was a mainstay in the band's repertoire, featuring the alto saxophone of Phil Woods.

Jones returned to the United States but would go back to Europe for one of the great musical adventures of his life.

Many new voices in composition would be heard in the 1960s, sometimes in surprising circumstances, and leaders such as Count Basie and Duke Ellington would continue to record and perform music that became classic. And one man who'd had an important big band in the 1940s would make a major comeback.

8

TOWARD A CONCERT ENSEMBLE

1960–1979

The next twenty years were turbulent in the jazz world. The pop music world experienced the British Invasion of groups like the Beatles and the Rolling Stones, folk rock artists such as Simon & Garfunkel and the Byrds, and then disco in the 1970s. Although several bands were quite active in the 1960s, many places where jazz could be heard either closed or changed musical format. Though jazz was still being recorded, small labels were bought by larger companies and promotion suffered.

The big band transitioned into the educational world. Gene Hall designed the first degree program in jazz at North Texas State Teachers College in 1947, and pioneering educators such as Clem DeRosa and Marshall Brown developed jazz programs in public schools in New York State. In 1959, Stan Kenton presented a clinic at Indiana University under the auspices of the National Stage Band Camps, in which he was joined by Johnny Richards, Russell Garcia, Buddy Baker, and many other professional instrumentalists and composer/arrangers. Such clinics continued during the 1960s with more residencies at different colleges. Such musicians as Mike Vax, Peter Erskine, Randy Brecker, and Keith Jarrett attended and later became jazz legends. With the proliferation of jazz degrees being offered in colleges, more bands were often heard in the university rather than in the professional setting.

By the late 1960s, inspired by the success of the Thad Jones–Mel Lewis ensemble, which had a regular gig on Monday nights at the

Village Vanguard in New York City, Monday nights became big band nights at clubs all over the country. Many were called "rehearsal" bands because they rarely played outside the club setting, union hall, or school auditorium, because they were often made up of amateurs and pros alike and because students brought their music and learned how to write on the job.

The big band format proved resilient, showcasing music of many different styles and directions, and transitioning more and more into a concert music ensemble. The rest of this book documents some of the incredible bands that made such impressive and innovative music and developed new soloists, some of whom became stars on their own. Some rehearsal bands became so popular that they toured the United States, and some even played at festivals overseas.

Gerry Mulligan was a saxophonist, composer, and arranger who was first seen and heard nationally as part of Gene Krupa's band in 1946 and 1947. His playing was not as developed as his writing, and he was soon off the bandstand, writing full time. Krupa bought and played all of his compositions and arrangements, even though he often argued with Mulligan about his advanced musical direction. Mulligan went on to write for the Elliot Lawrence band in Philadelphia, and Gil Evans was so impressed that he recommended Mulligan move to New York, where he got him work writing for Claude Thornhill. Mulligan was one of the key architects of the Miles Davis Nonet from 1948 to 1950, and that ensemble recorded several of his compositions. Moving to Los Angeles after writing for Charlie Parker, Mulligan wrote for Stan Kenton as well as assembling a pioneering quartet with Chet Baker that did not have a piano. After touring internationally, Mulligan was back in New York and formed more small groups. But he always loved big bands and wanted one of his own. Called the Gerry Mulligan Concert Jazz Band, it was made up of all-star musicians handpicked by Mulligan and valve trombonist Bob Brookmeyer.

What: "All about Rosie" by George Russell
Where: Webster Hall, 125 East 11th Street, New York
When: July 10–11, 1961

George Russell originally wrote "All about Rosie" for the 1957 Brandeis University Festival of the Arts as a work for chamber ensemble; it was subsequently recorded for Columbia Records on June 10 and 20, 1957. It became a classic example of jazz in a concert music setting, which began as early as the Paul Whiteman, Artie Shaw, and Stan Kenton bands; such music was now called "Third Stream." Bill Evans's piano solo has been transcribed and studied in music classes all over the world. When Mulligan commissioned Russell to write for his Concert Jazz Band, Russell brought in a big band version of "All about Rosie," and Mulligan later said, "I nearly died!"

"All about Rosie" is based on an Alabama children's song/game "Rosie, Little Rosie." Russell wrote this work as a three-movement suite. The first is in a medium-fast tempo as we hear the melody (0:09), which then develops as new melodies based on the original are added and expanded, playing against each other with a rhythmic figure playing underneath. The movement ends abruptly.

The second movement is slower and bluesy (2:12), with instruments playing either solo or in duet (baritone and tenor sax, flute and trombone, etc.). This culminates in duets with tenor and baritone saxes (3:21) and two trombones playing complementary lines against each other (3:47), later joined by cup-muted trumpets (4:17).

The cymbal introduces movement three (5:21), where we once again hear the melody paraphrased as the background builds in intensity. It is in this movement that the piece breaks out for improvised solos (there was a cut made in the original score for time purposes): Mulligan (6:46), Brookmeyer (7:42), trumpeter Don Ferrara (8:09), and alto saxophonist Gene Quill (8:49) are featured. The movement ends by repeating the end of movement one (9:15).

Many historians point to the superiority of the Evans piano solo and thus choose the chamber ensemble version as the best, but historian Bill Kirchner considers the Mulligan Concert Jazz Band recording the definitive version based on the excellence of all of the solos, the "bottom" supplied by Gene Allen's baritone sax and bass clarinet, and par-

ticularly the exciting drumming of Mel Lewis. I invite you to choose on
your own.

Mulligan's ensemble lasted until 1964, when, in Kirchner's words, it
"simply ceased working, though it never seems to have come to an
official end." Mulligan went on to lead several excellent groups over the
years. He composed works for symphony orchestra and chamber ensembles and played with all sorts of musicians, including Buddhist
monks. I was fortunate to work with him in 1995. His library is now
housed at the Library of Congress. Mulligan passed away in 1996.

Maynard Ferguson led a band in the mid-1940s as a teenager in his
native Montreal, Canada, and word soon spread of this prodigy who
played both reed and brass instruments. His range on the trumpet was
astounding, and unlike many high-note players, his low register was
equally beautiful. It didn't take long for American bandleaders to con-
vince him to move to the United States, where he played with Jimmy
Dorsey, Boyd Raeburn, and Charlie Barnet. In 1950, Ferguson joined
the Stan Kenton Innovations Orchestra, and a piece was specifically
written for him by Shorty Rogers. He remained with Kenton until 1953,
when he joined the studio orchestra at Paramount Pictures, playing on
at least forty-six soundtracks. He continued to play jazz gigs while with
Paramount and finally left to play jazz full time in 1956. Invited to lead
a big band at New York's jazz club Birdland, Ferguson recorded two
albums with this all-star ensemble. He went back to the West Coast and
put together a full-time touring band of young musicians. Willie Maid-
en and "Slide" Hampton both played in the orchestra and arranged.

**What: "Sometimes I Feel Like a Motherless Child," traditional;
arranged by Slide Hampton
Where: Capitol Recording Studios, 146 West 46th Street, New
York
When: March 15, 1960**

A short, symphonic-sounding concert piece with no improvisation, this
is an example of how composers for big bands took the opportunities
offered to write more ambitious music. The treatment of this African
American spiritual is in rubato tempo (it is not in strict time) and re-

minds us that this piece is quite often sung by an a cappella choir (a vocal group with no accompaniment). Hampton wrote this in memory of his mother, who'd passed away shortly before.

Ferguson's ensemble was made up of four trumpets (Maynard being one, although he often played valve trombone, French horn, and baritone horn), two trombones, four saxophones, piano, bass, and drums, but it sounds bigger than its size would suggest.

Ferguson's band lasted until 1965. He toured with a sextet but moved to England with his family after a few years. He put together another big band there and returned to the United States, where he led a successful unit for the rest of his life. His band has the distinction of having a record at number twenty-two on the *Billboard* pop charts during the 1970s—Bill Conti's "Gonna Fly Now" from the motion picture *Rocky*.

Harry James was still leading a band in Las Vegas during the 1950s and 1960s. Though he still played his old hits and new pop and country songs, his band was heavily influenced by Count Basie's New Testament band, and he even hired Basie arrangers Thad Jones and Ernie Wilkins to write most of his ensemble's new book.

What: "The Jazz Connoisseur" by Ernie Wilkins
Where: Los Angeles
When: January 19, 1961

The rhythm section of pianist Jack Percival, guitarist Terry Rosen, bassist Russ Phillips, and drummer Tony DiNicola plays a short introduction, then the AABA piece begins with two tenor saxes and James playing the melody. Like Basie, James featured "dueling" tenor saxophones that traded solos—Sam Firmature (0:51) and Modesto Briseno (an extremely talented musician who died tragically too young) (1:11). James's solo once again reminds us of his great improvisational skills, as well as his huge sound and excellent technique (1:36). If one listens closely, there's a splice right before the saxophone soli (the saxophone section gets a chance to play in harmony with the rhythm section), an example of the new freedom in recordings made possible by using the best sections of multiple performances (2:00). The full band plays (2:39), and then the melody returns as in the beginning of the record (3:02).

James led his band into the 1980s until his death from cancer at the age of sixty-seven. It was always an excellent unit, playing an eclectic book of music. James's attitude was that if he liked something, he played it regardless of popularity or style.

When we last met up with Quincy Jones, he was in Europe writing, arranging, and studying music. Returning to the states, he was immediately signed to a recording contract with Mercury Records and acquired an agent who encouraged him to put a band together. After recording two albums, an opportunity to become musical director of a show called *Free and Easy* allowed him to bring the band on a European show tour that was to culminate in the show opening on Broadway. Unfortunately, the show closed and the band was stranded in Europe. Jones had many contacts thanks to his years there, and he put a tour together that lasted seven months. It is a tribute to his humanity and excellence as a musician that almost all of the musicians remained with the group.

What: "Meet B. B." by Quincy Jones
Where: Newport Jazz Festival, Rhode Island
When: July 3, 1961

When Jones brought the band back to the states, he had a hard time keeping it together due to lack of bookings. The band played another series of concerts in Europe (happily, recordings of some of them are available), and the performance at the Newport Jazz Festival, where this track comes from, turned out to be one of the group's last public appearances.

"Meet B. B." is in AABA form and was written for expatriate trumpeter Benny Bailey and was first played by the Harry Arnold Orchestra of Sweden. Bailey stayed in Europe after a 1955 tour with the Lionel Hampton band and was always busy playing gigs there. Bailey played with Jones's band when that ensemble played its first tour and had to be replaced when the band returned. Joe Newman (who'd just left the Count Basie band) takes the wonderful solo here. Notice the use of the piccolo and muted trumpet lead, a unique color that immediately identified the Jones ensemble (0:10).

The Jones band made an excellent album for Impulse Records late in the year, which proved to be a strong farewell for this ensemble. Jones remained in New York composing, arranging, and producing recordings for Mercury Records and was promoted to vice president in 1964, the first black executive with a major record label. Although he is known today primarily for his work with Michael Jackson, his big band career is one of the highlights of 1960s jazz.

After Thad Jones left Count Basie, he freelanced and wrote a lot of music for the Harry James band, much of which was never recorded but has recently been published. Count Basie hired him to write enough music for an album to be called *Count Basie Plays Thad Jones*. Jones's new music was too advanced for the Basie band. Count cancelled the album, but allowed Jones to keep the music. Thad and drummer Mel Lewis called a rehearsal of top-notch studio pros (many of whom were on staff at the CBS, ABC, and NBC radio and television networks) to play this music, which led to more new music written and more rehearsals held. Although the rehearsals were private, guests sometimes showed up, including a jazz DJ named Alan Grant. Grant was so impressed with what he heard that he persuaded Village Vanguard owner Max Gordon to let the band play there for a couple of Monday nights (clubs with live music usually did poorly on Mondays or were closed altogether). The first performance of "The Jazz Band" took place on February 7, 1966, and the Vanguard was packed with enthusiastic listeners. Historians now consider the Thad Jones–Mel Lewis Orchestra to be one of the most exciting and influential ensembles of all time.

What: "Don't Git Sassy" by Thad Jones
Where: Village Vanguard, 178 7th Avenue South, New York
When: April 28, 1967

A bluesy melody with a shuffle beat (the phrase used to describe it in jazz terms is *downhome*), this is exciting and infectious music, basic yet harmonically innovative, and as in most of Jones's music, there's plenty of space for soloists—veterans such as pianist Sir Roland Hanna (Benny Goodman, Charles Mingus, Wynton Marsalis) (0:11), trumpeters Snooky Young (Jimmie Lunceford, Count Basie, Gerald Wilson, the *Tonight Show* band) (2:12), and Jimmy Nottingham (Lionel Hampton, Count Basie, Charlie Barnet) (3:16), both using plunger mutes, and newer musicians such as tenor saxophonist Joe Farrell, who later played flute with Chick Corea, Aretha Franklin, and Santana (4:15). After the solos, the saxophone section gets a workout all its own (5:52). Notice the lead sax is a soprano, not an alto as in most big bands. Jones helped to popularize this sound and it became an identifying feature of the Jones–Lewis ensemble.

Although Jones did not write rock music very often, "Us" certainly qualifies. It often opened live appearances where it would be extended for solos.

What: "Us" by Thad Jones
Where: A & R Studios, 799 7th Avenue, New York
When: May 25, 1970

After a fanfare-like brass figure, Jerome Richardson solos on soprano saxophone (0:11). The melody is in brass with no rhythmic accompaniment, sounding like a gospel piece (0:38). After a transition (1:09), the bass line joined by guitar indicates a key change (1:13), and an entirely new melody in unison is heard (1:30), which becomes louder and more complex (2:03). After another key change, we are back in the original key, and the first melody is played by brass again, with a short ending (3:00).

Jones's music quickly became the most popular new music played by rehearsal bands and school ensembles throughout the world, as it represented old and new values—swing plus harmonic innovation (Jones became perhaps the most influential arranger in the jazz world after 1970; his music has been the subject of textbooks, theses, and musicological studies).

This ensemble toured and recorded extensively (there are many television appearances available on YouTube), but in 1979, Jones left the band abruptly and moved to Copenhagen; he later led the Count Basie Orchestra. Lewis carried on (the joke at the time was "Thad and

Mel got a divorce, and Mel got to keep the kids") as the band became a breeding ground for new musicians and new music. Lewis died in 1990, but the band continues as the Vanguard Jazz Orchestra, playing Monday nights, touring, and recording.

Gerald Wilson spent the 1950s writing for a variety of acts and shows and leading a big band for an occasional live appearance. In 1961, he signed a deal with producer Albert Marx, who made a release agreement with Richard Bock, owner of the Pacific Jazz label. Wilson made ten albums for Marx and Bock between 1961 and 1969, playing contemporary jazz standards as well as new compositions by Wilson and other band members. A few of the new compositions became standards in their own right.

What: "Viva Tirado" by Gerald Wilson
Where: Pacific Jazz Studios, Los Angeles
When: August 27, 1962

Wilson was a great fan of bullfighting, and this composition was written in honor of Jose Ramon Tirado, a matador that Wilson particularly admired. The piece is in ABA form, and features an early recording of legendary guitarist Joe Pass. Trumpeter Carmell Jones would live and work in Europe for fifteen years before returning to play and teach in his native Kansas City, Kansas (1:17); tenor saxophonist Teddy Edwards had played with Charlie Parker and made a famous recording with tenor saxophonist Dexter Gordon called *The Duel* (2:21). Pass has another solo (3:25), and then the band plays the last chorus (4:26). Mel Lewis is the drummer.

Wilson's ensembles became known for featuring established players such as Bud Shank and Al Porcino, as well as younger players. Wilson always listened to contemporary music and recorded such rock songs as "Light My Fire" and "California Soul." Yet Wilson suffered the same fate as many leaders: key musicians could not tour with him, and he didn't want to go out on the road with substitutes, so his ensemble remained primarily a West Coast attraction.

Stan Kenton was never one to stand still, and his ensembles continued to play powerful, innovative music. As discussed earlier, Stan had two French horns in his band in 1956, but the response of the instrument (in generating a sound) was not as fast as trumpets and trombones, and they were dropped. In 1960, he added four musicians playing a new instrument called a mellophonium, a variant on the mellophone. Mellophones were sometimes used in dance bands in the 1920s (there's a picture of the Paul Whitemen trumpet section in which the musicians have them), but they never really caught on. This instrument was originally meant to substitute for French horns in marching bands, as the bell of the mellophone is forward rather than backward as on French horns. The first mellophoniums were manufactured by Conn in 1957, and representatives of the instrument company contacted Kenton. Kenton liked the instrument and, after making some design suggestions in consultation with Gene Roland and Johnny Richards, added a section of four of them to his orchestra. Almost immediately, it was discovered that the instrument had problems sounding in tune (some said because of the design changes), but they added a nice color to the Kenton Orchestra until the ensemble disbanded in 1963.

Kenton

What: "Tonight" by Stephen Sondheim and Leonard Bernstein; arranged by Johnny Richards
Where: Goldwyn Studios, Los Angeles
When: March 15, 1961

There's a Kenton piano solo (0:39) and then one bathes in the lush brass sound of the four mellophoniums, three tenor and two bass trombones, tuba, alto sax, two tenor saxes, baritone and bass sax, five trumpets (although the music was so taxing that two trumpets were hired to substitute during the recording sessions), bass, drums, and three percussionists. The last minute of this track is sheer sonic luxury, with the entire ensemble playing with no vibrato but with a rich sound. Piano ends the track as it began (3:15).

Producer Lee Gillette played the entire album for the producers of the movie version of "West Side Story," and they were very impressed, even implying that the Kenton ensemble might have been part of the soundtrack if the filmmakers knew that the music could sound like that.

The album turned out to be important for Kenton, resulting in a best seller and the first of two Grammy Awards for the band. Even composer Leonard Bernstein loved the album and went to hear the band play this music when they performed in New York.

Trumpeter Don Ellis graduated from Boston University with a degree in music composition then went into the army, where he met such future jazz stars as pianist Cedar Walton and saxophonists Don Menza and Eddie Harris. He later played in the Glenn Miller ghost band and with Maynard Ferguson. Attracted to more modern music, he was soon sharing bandstands with Charles Mingus, Eric Dolphy, and George Russell. He also appeared as a soloist with the New York Philharmonic in a nationally televised concert.

Moving to the West Coast, he began studying Indian music and formed the Hindustani Jazz Sextet, and also led a workshop big band with music in unusual rhythms as found in Indian, Greek, Bulgarian, and other ethnic music; instead of music in 2, 3, and 4, Ellis's compositions were in 5, 7, 9, 13, and other odd meters. With continual rehearsal, the musicians came to play his challenging music with ease, and a residency at a club named Bonesville in Los Angeles created positive word-of-mouth. Ellis asked enthusiastic fans to write letters to the management of the Monterey Jazz Festival to request the band perform there. The campaign succeeded, and the band's appearance at the 1966 festival created a sensation. Here was a band that straddled both jazz and rock (the band often performed in rock clubs), and its appeal was cross-generational, from older fans to rock listeners. Ellis's band included five saxophones, four trumpets, three trombones, three percussion, and two acoustic basses. It also featured electric Fender Rhodes piano and electric bass, new to big bands.

What: "Indian Lady" by Don Ellis
Where: Stanford University, Palo Alto, California
When: August 5, 1968

This was the band's closer during this period, and there are many recordings of it available, including a powerful version from Tanglewood, a summer music festival in Massachusetts. This live version has one of

Ellis's most experimental and fun solos played on an electronic trumpet that enabled him to get many different sounds as well as to amplify the instrument (1:22). Pete Robinson solos on electric piano (5:15), followed by Glenn Ferris on trombone, both playing "out there" (6:26). Not to be outdone, tenor saxophonists John Klemmer and John Falzone have a "battle" (8:03), and the excitement and intensity just keep growing (it says a lot for Ellis that Klemmer had a promising solo career but joined the Ellis band for the opportunity to play this music). Listening to these two soloists interact is frightening, as they seem to anticipate each other. The highlight of this solo exchange is when they generate a Dixieland pseudo-waltz that drives the audience crazy (11:12). A duet between drummer Ralph Humphrey and percussionist Gene Strimling keeps the momentum going (12:37) until the band comes back in to repeat the AABA melody (14:12). Just when you think the piece is over, Ellis returns with an exciting solo (15:36) as the band builds up momentum again for a crashing finish.

The Ellis ensemble did it all, presenting music that was a fusion of the old and the new and featuring excellent soloists who took the music to different places at every performance. Plus, there are very few big bands in history who could generate such intense excitement live. Audiences and musicians have written that Ellis concerts were powerful events that remained in their memories for years, similar to reactions of Grateful Dead concertgoers.

Ellis continued to explore and modify his orchestra—in 1971, he added an electrified string quartet and Bulgarian Milcho Leviev, who could freely improvise in the most complex of musical environments. Ellis also composed the music for the motion picture *The French Connection*. He nearly died from heart problems in 1975 but was back leading a new orchestra in 1976. Unfortunately, his heart problems persisted and he died in 1978 at the age of forty-four.

Ellis proved that there was far more that could be explored in the world of the big band and particularly that new, often experimental music could appeal to a wide audience of all ages. His music was published and has been studied and performed by high school and college jazz ensembles all over the world. At one time difficult to play by seasoned professionals, this music is now often read at sight by students.

Clare Fischer graduated from Michigan State University wi[ ]
music in 1955. He was soon playing and writing for the inte[ ]
known vocal group, the Hi-Los. Moving to Los Angeles in[ ]
1960s, he played Latin and Brazilian music with Cal Tjader[ ]
Gilberto and became a well-respected pianist who made several albums
as a soloist and leader of small groups. As an arranger, he wrote an
impressive album for trumpeter Donald Byrd and strings in 1957 that
wasn't released until many years later. But an album of Duke Ellington
compositions arranged for Dizzy Gillespie in 1960 gained Fischer wide
attention. In 1968, Fischer put together a band that played in clubs in
Los Angeles and made two now-legendary albums.

What: "Miles Behind" by Clare Fischer
Where: T. T. G. Studios, 1441 North McCadden Place, Los
Angeles
When: October 9, 1968

This is a piece in a fast tempo in seven, and we can immediately hear an
ensemble of warm, deep instrumental colors—five trumpets, four trombones, two alto saxophones, two tenor saxophones, baritone and bass
saxophone, electric piano, bass, and drums (0:44). The melody is sixteen
bars long and is repeated before soloists commence. Warne Marsh (a
greatly underrated soloist) takes a solo on tenor saxophone (1:27), and
Conte Candoli plays a trumpet solo (2:07). After these solos, Fischer
shows off his composing abilities when the band plays a fantasia of an
accompanying figure that moves from reeds to brass (3:03), getting
louder and then subsiding with low instruments sounding a dissonant
chord (4:08). When the melody returns, it is playfully performed by
flutes and muted trumpets (4:34). The track ends with a clarinet over
muted brass.

Fischer would go on to lead an ensemble called Salsa Picante, which
included a group of singers. He would be nominated for eleven Grammy awards for various projects, winning three times. Much of his later
work involved arranging for pop and R&B artists such as Prince, Robert
Palmer, Paul McCartney, and Michael Jackson. His son Brent Fischer
is a bassist and percussionist who has arranged for Toni Braxton, Elvis
Costello, Prince, and Michael Jackson.

Gary McFarland taught himself to play piano and vibraphone and reportedly did not know how to read music until he attended Berklee College of Music. He quickly learned how to write for big bands (writer/lyricist Gene Lees called him "an adult prodigy") and called up trombonist Bob Brookmeyer to show him a piece he'd written. At the time, Brookmeyer was co-leader of Gerry Mulligan's Concert Jazz Band and brought McFarland and the score to the next rehearsal. McFarland's music was played and the band liked it. Soon after, McFarland was getting all sorts of dates as an instrumentalist and arranger.

What: "Manha de Carnaval" (Morning of Carnaval) by Carl Sigman and Luiz Bonfa; arranged by Gary McFarland
Where: Columbia 30th Street Studio, New York
When: August 28, 1962

This track comes from one of Stan Getz's loveliest albums, *Big Band Bossa Nova*. This melody is a theme from the motion picture *Black Orpheus*, and once English lyrics were written by Carl Sigman, the song became known as "A Day in the Life of a Fool." Along with "The Girl from Ipanema," this song introduced the bossa nova genre to American audiences, and many artists were performing and covering these songs during this period.

Beside Getz, guitarist Jim Hall is featured, and it is his guitar freely playing that opens the track. When Getz begins, the ensemble of three trumpets, two trombones, French horn, five reeds, Hall's guitar, piano, bass, drums, and two percussion also comes in, with mixed reeds and brass playing offbeat figures (0:36). McFarland also takes the melody and varies the rhythm (1:22), leading to another Hall solo (1:35). The melody returns in the trumpets as Hank Jones plays a brief piano solo before Getz returns (2:32). Unison trumpets return playing a variant of the melody (4:13) and then restate it as Jones plays fills. The track recaps the beginning with Getz playing the melody with woodwind offbeats (5:00) and ends softly.

McFarland is now considered a major figure in jazz, folk, and pop rock, as he recorded jazz-tinged albums that had treatments of Beatles songs and other pop songs of the era, one of the first arrangers to do so.

In 1968, he recorded an innovative album entitled *A_* *ful* for his own Skye record label that presages the music of the 1970s, and he would no doubt have ~~of that musical world. But on November 2, 1971, he w~~ a record date, and a high dose of methadone was added leading to a heart attack and death.

who?

In 1960, Gil Evans led an ensemble that was resident at the Jazz Gallery in New York, where he began a new phase of his music approach—letting the musicians develop the music on the stand during the gig. His music became less formal and provided more space for improvisation. Missing from the music scene during most of the 1960s to raise his children, Evans returned with a new jazz-rock orchestra, which was attractive to younger listeners while alienating much of his older audience. He became friends with Jimi Hendrix and planned a concert and album with the legendary guitarist, who passed away before the concert could be realized. Evans made the album shortly thereafter.

What: "Up from the Skies" by Jimi Hendrix; arranged by Gil Evans
Where: New York
When: June 7, 1974

Evans once again proves a master of combining instrumental colors, creating new musical frameworks, and adding improvisation to the mix. The track is a series of statements of the jazzy Hendrix melody with a walking bass under an ensemble of clarinets of various sizes, synthesizers, and sometimes marimba (0:13) that is loose enough so that these statements come and go with solos in between, allowing the form of the music to go in many directions. Guitarists John Abercrombie and Ryo Kawasaki trade solos with electronic effects (2:06), and several musicians double on synthesizer.

"I write popular music," was how Evans described what he was doing, and when he played gigs, he laid down a basic musical framework and then let his musicians run with it. The ensemble played a weekly gig at Sweet Basil's in Greenwich Village, New York, and made worldwide tours of summer jazz festivals with all-star musicians. Evans also posed and arranged music for the motion pictures *The Color of ₁ney* and *Absolute Beginners*. He died in 1988.

At a time when there were few new big bands with extensive touring schedules and record contracts, drummer Buddy Rich had both months after he left the Harry James Orchestra in 1965. He was a veteran of the Artie Shaw and Tommy Dorsey orchestras and led his own excellent orchestra from 1946 to 1948 but gave it up to tour with *Jazz at the Philharmonic*, a traveling jazz show produced by Norman Granz. In 1966, his new big band played clubs in Los Angeles, where it was heard by the top show business personalities of the day. Rich appeared on *The Tonight Show Starring Johnny Carson* plugging his band, and dazzled audiences by his outsized personality and virtuoso drumming. Determined to lead a contemporary band that appealed to younger audiences, he played high-powered jazz along with contemporary songs in clubs, high schools, and colleges; much of his band personnel were recent graduates of North Texas State (now the University of North Texas) and Berklee College of Music.

What: "New Blues" by Don Piestrup
Where: Pacific Jazz Studios, Los Angeles
When: June 16, 1967

Piestrup spent most of his professional life in the commercial music field but wrote some wonderful music for the Rich band. This is another example of a trend in big band music that was being exploited: creating different sonic color groups instead of writing for instrumental sections. "New Blues" is an attractive melody played by flutes, alto sax, and muted trumpets (0:11) with accompanying figures played by either tenor saxes or muted brass (0:39). Ray Starling plays an attractive piano solo (Starling also played mellophonium with Stan Kenton's Orchestra) (0:16), and Jay Corre plays a beautiful solo on tenor sax (2:25). Piestrup writes a variant of his bluesy melody played by trumpets and saxes (3:25) then by the entire band, which is the climax of the piece. The original melody returns to end the composition (4:19).

Rich continued to tour across the world until his death in 1987. At this writing, Piestrup leads a rehearsal band in the San Francisco area.

Pianist Duke Pearson was born in Atlanta, Georgia, and took up the trumpet, later switching to piano. He was head of A&R at Blue Note Records and recorded and produced several albums for the label. In 1967, he formed a big band of top New York session players, recorded two albums, and played gigs on the East Coast.

What: "New Girl" by Duke Pearson
Where: Rudy Van Gelder Studios, 445 Sylvan Avenue,
Englewood Cliffs, New Jersey
When: December 15, 1967

An introduction in three begins this piece, which is in standard four swing. After the melody is stated (0:09), solos by Burt Collins (0:49) and Lew Tabackin follow (2:40) with a piano solo by Pearson (3:52). Collins returns (4:30) and the band plays a final chorus with exciting drumming from Mickey Roker (5:12).

Pearson was diagnosed with multiple sclerosis and returned to Georgia where he died in 1980. His big band's reputation has grown in stature, and publications of his music are top sellers.

Drummer Kenny Clarke is considered an innovator in the drumming world for the development of a new style in the 1940s, wherein the actual time was played on the cymbal, allowing the snare and bass drum to be used for additional figures such as offbeat accents. In the mid-1940s he was the house drummer for a club called Minton's Playhouse, where the earliest experimentation of the new jazz called bebop took place; regular attendees were Charlie Parker and Dizzy Gillespie. He was the original drummer of the Modern Jazz Quartet, which included pianist John Lewis and vibraharpist Milt Jackson. After visiting France on and off since the late 1940s, he finally moved there in 1956, where he worked with European and American musicians across the continent.

Self-taught Belgian pianist and arranger Francois Boland lived and wrote in the United States for many years, where he was a protégé of pianist Mary Lou Williams. He worked with Count Basie, Benny Goodman, and Chet Baker and returned to Europe to write for the Kurt Edelhagen band.

In 1961, Italian producer Gigi Campi approached Clarke and Boland to form an all-star big band for recording, but the ensemble began limited touring in 1966. The musicians took pride in the fact that they were as good or better than the finest big bands in the United States, but the sheer logistics of bringing these busy musicians together to rehearse and perform as much as they did were made smoother thanks to Campi's tenacity. In addition to top musicians from England, France, and Sweden, many expatriate Americans joined over the years, such as tenor saxophonists Johnny Griffin and Eddie "Lockjaw" Davis, alto saxophonists Herb Geller and Phil Woods, baritone saxophonist Sahib Shihab, bassist Jimmy Woode, trombonist Nat Peck, and trumpeters Idrees Sulieman and Benny Bailey.

What: "Griff's Groove" by Francois "Francy" Boland
Where: Ronnie Scott's, 47 Frith Street, Soho, London
When: February 28, 1969

From a live gig at one of the top clubs in Europe, this recording has become a classic. A blues first played by harmonized saxes provides the framework for solos by Griffin (be sure to listen closely for his "Rhapsody in Blue" reference) (4:20) and Bailey (5:11). Besides the powerful ensemble sound, what is unique about this band is that it features not one but two drummers: Kenny Clarke and British drummer Kenny Clare. It speaks to their excellence as musicians that both intersperse accents and other figures without getting in each other's way.

This ensemble made fifteen albums and was featured on radio and television throughout Europe (there are many extraordinary performances available on YouTube, including a concert with singer Carmen McRae). A proposed U.S. tour did not work out, to the disappointment of everyone connected with the band. When alto saxophonist Derek Humble died in 1971 after several years of poor health, the musicians did not want to continue and the group dissolved.

Sun Ra began life as Herman Blount and spent his early years in Birmingham, Alabama, playing piano and organizing big bands. He joined the Fletcher Henderson Orchestra as pianist and arranger in 1946. In 1952 he changed his name to Le Sony'r Ra and led a group called the Space Trio.

Fascinated by Egyptian culture and science fiction, by 1952 Sun Ra came to believe that he had been abducted by UFOs and had visited the planet Saturn. By the late 1950s, his ensembles performed in unusual costumes and headdresses. Upon moving to New York in 1966, the Arkestra played a regular Monday night gig at Slug's Saloon, where it attracted a great deal of both positive and negative attention. By 1968, the ensemble lived communally in a house in Philadelphia, which was Sun Ra's home base for the rest of his life. Sun Ra wrote extensively about his interests and beliefs over the years, and these were also featured in the lyrics of his songs. They included black nationalism, kabbalah, freemasonry, and Egyptian mysticism.

Sun Ra described his music as cosmic jazz, which changed and adapted over the years. Clearly influenced by classic big band jazz, bebop, and free jazz (a style of jazz often without a steady pulse, utilizing various sounds such as overblowing a saxophone, and a looser harmonic framework). The Arkestra also featured extensive use of percussion, multiple electronic keyboards, and tape delay (Robert Moog gave Sun Ra an early prototype of his Minimoog). During the late 1960s, the ensemble was made up of thirty musicians, dancers, and fire-eaters, and live performances featured elaborate lighting. By the 1970s, the Arkestra played Jelly Roll Morton and Fletcher Henderson compositions in addition to its original repertoire; Sun Ra believed that he should remind audiences of the jazz tradition, as he felt that they were not aware of their culture.

What: "King Porter Stomp" by Jelly Roll Morton; arranged by Sun Ra
Where: Storyville, New York
When: October 24 or 29, 1977

Although Sun Ra made many records as a pianist and a bandleader, his live performances were where audiences could fully experience his ensembles. As discussed, the band's repertoire was made of Ra's unusual compositions, standard songs, and jazz classics. "King Porter Stomp" gets an almost surreal workout here, with the band stomping as if it was playing for a dance, and many people soloing. Most are unidentified, but the tenor sax solo is by longtime Sun Ra bandmember John Gilmore (1:38), who'd played with the leader for forty years. Sun Ra plays a keyboard called the rocksichord, and this unusual color reminds us that this is no 1930s re-creation. The track's energy is infectious, bringing new life to the piece.

Sun Ra passed away in 1993, but his orchestra continues to concertize. Like many musicians with original ideas, his recordings continue to inspire artists of many disciplines.

Toshiko Akiyoshi was discovered by Oscar Peterson when he heard her play jazz piano in Japan. She received a scholarship to Berklee College of Music and has had a successful career as a soloist and leader of small groups. Married to flautist/tenor saxophonist Lew Tabackin, they put together a big band on the West Coast in March 1973 that recorded for JVC (Japanese Victor); some albums were later released in the United States. They toured extensively in Japan.

What: "Henpecked Old Man" by Toshiko Akiyoshi
Where: Monterey Jazz Festival, Monterey, California
When: 1975

This is a blues with special guest Clark Terry on flugelhorn. Lew Tabackin solos on tenor sax as well (2:14). The full ensemble takes over (4:00) on a wild ride until Tabackin returns to solo (5:07).

Akiyoshi and Tabackin eventually moved to the East Coast and Toshiko played gigs with small bands so that she could keep the new big band together. They had a regular Monday night gig at Birdland for several years, but Toshiko eventually disbanded to concentrate on playing solo piano.

In 1964, Billy Strayhorn became ill with esophageal cancer and died in 1967. His last composition was composed in the hospital and delivered to the Ellington band.

What: "Blood Count" by Billy Strayhorn
Where: New York, New York
When: August 28, 1967

A solo for Johnny Hodges, perhaps Strayhorn's favorite voice in the Ellington orchestra, this is a disturbing last work.

Ellington was devastated, but he continued to write music and tour. A triumphal seventieth birthday concert tour featured organist "Wild Bill" Davis playing a piece that had become a standard.

What: "Satin Doll" by Johnny Mercer, Billy Strayhorn, and Duke Ellington
Where: Colston Hall, Bristol, England
When: November 25, 1969

Davis is the main soloist in an arrangement that is flashier and played faster than the original version discussed in chapter 7.

The story of Chris McGregor highlights how big bands and jazz were fully an international movement by the 1960s. It also speaks of this pianist and arranger's courage and conviction to write and perform music his way despite deterrents that would have stopped many other musicians.

McGregor was born and raised in South Africa, where he heard African traditional music that permeated his own improvisational and compositional style. He became a student at the South African College of Music and was exposed to both concert music and jazz. Playing in show pit orchestras and jazz festivals, he met a wide range of musicians and put together a sextet called the Blue Notes. As the white leader of a mostly black group, the musicians were harassed repeatedly by police, as South Africa's apartheid laws segregated the white and nonwhite populations. In 1964, the Blue Notes left South Africa and played all over Europe, switching direction toward more free jazz. Subsequently McGregor put together a big band in England in 1967 that was resident at the Old Place (which later became one of the leading jazz clubs in the world, Ronnie Scott's) and was well reviewed in the British music press. In 1969, McGregor reorganized this group of South African expatriate and young British jazz musicians as the Brotherhood of Breath, which blended South African tribal music and blues. Its recordings were praised in the European jazz press; alas, few of them were heard in the United States until many years later. The band was also well received at European jazz festivals and other live gigs. McGregor was compared to Duke Ellington in that he gathered an ensemble of unusual musical personalities and wrote music taking their strengths and weaknesses into consideration; the resulting ensemble sounds were striking, unusual, yet accessible and resonated with audiences. As crazy as the music sometimes got, it was danceable and happy.

What: "The Bride" by Dudu Pukwana; arranged by Chris McGregor
Where: London
When: January 9, 1971

An infectious, exciting rhythm is set up, and then we hear a group of musical lines going back and forth through the ensemble (0:32), leading to a John Surman solo on soprano sax (Surman became one of the leading lights in British jazz who drew inspiration from folk music) (2:04). A band background brings the ensemble back (3:52), and Surman continues as we hear a repeat of the beginning of the piece (5:00), leading to Surman and the rhythm section again (5:34). The band repeats the beginning of the piece (6:16), leading to an explosive ending. In live settings, new musical lines were set up by McGregor or perhaps another musician, and an expansion of the piece was created on the spot, similar to Gil Evans's approach with his 1960 Jazz Gallery ensemble.

Like so many bandleaders, McGregor had trouble keeping the band together due to lack of work. The group would record an album, play a series of concerts, and then disband. McGregor played solo piano or toured with small groups in between his big band activity. However, the world music scene was growing during the 1980s, highlighted by Paul Simon's *Graceland* album from 1986, and interest in McGregor's ensemble grew; in 1989, American tenor saxophonist Archie Shepp played a series of successful concerts with the Brotherhood of Breath. Unfortunately, McGregor passed away of cancer in 1990. Since then, the

Brotherhood of Breath has been acknowledged as a pioneering ensemble of many different styles of jazz, folk, and urban music. More and more European composers would use the folk music of their different cities and countries as source music for compositions and improvisation.

Charles Mingus led various small groups after moving to New York; they were always called the Jazz Workshop. He recorded many classic albums and featured musicians who became legendary such as alto saxophonist/flautist Eric Dolphy, trombonist Jimmy Knepper, alto saxophonists John Handy, Charles MacPherson, and Jackie McLean, pianist Mal Waldron, tenor saxophonists Booker Ervin and Bobby Jones, saxophonist Roland Kirk, baritone saxophonists Pepper Adams and Jerome Richardson, and drummer Dannie Richmond.

In 1971, Mingus recorded an album with a large ensemble entitled *Let My Children Hear Music*; it featured music that had been written as early as 1939. Assisting him in notating and orchestrating the music were Alan Raph and Sy Johnson. Mingus would later say that this was one of his favorite albums.

What: "Don't Be Afraid, the Clown's Afraid Too" by Charles Mingus; transcribed, arranged, and orchestrated by Sy Johnson; conducted by Teo Macero
Where: New York
When: September–December 1972

To even attempt to describe this music would be foolish, so it's best to just sit back and let the world of Charles Mingus envelop you. The liner notes to *Let My Children Hear Music* provide insight into Mingus's thoughts on this project, and they may be found through the following link: http://mingusmingusmingus.com/mingus/what-is-a-jazz-composer.

A veteran of the Stan Kenton and Maynard Ferguson ensembles as trombonist and arranger, Don Sebesky subsequently arranged and conducted for many pop and jazz artists. He has been nominated for eleven Grammy awards, winning three.

What: "Free As a Bird" by Don Sebesky
Where: Rudy Van Gelder Studios, 445 Sylvan Avenue,
Englewood Cliffs, New Jersey
When: April–May 1973

A feature for pianist Bob James, soprano saxophonist Grover Washington Jr., flugelhorn player Freddie Hubbard, and Sebesky himself on electric piano, this very fast track is dominated by "warm" brass: flugelhorns (instead of trumpets), French horns, and baritone horns (which have been described as small tubas, which, like their larger counterparts, yield a big, warm sound when played). The incredible bass playing by Ron Carter and the drumming of Jack DeJohnette are also featured (note the use of the accordion in the ensemble right before the statement of the melody; Sebesky plays this as well).

From 1980 on, new composers would bring many more new approaches to big bands, with some veterans still very much active. The next chapter continues the story.

9

LIMITLESS POSSIBILITIES

1980 and Beyond

There was good news and bad news on the big band front after 1980. The good news was that new bands formed, new writers continued to bring fresh and sometimes quite unusual ideas to the big band format, audiences continued to support them in clubs and concerts, jazz programs in high schools and colleges continued to flourish, and many bands recorded and spread their music throughout the globe. The bad news is that big bands rarely toured (except for festivals and concerts) and the musicians who populated them played many other gigs besides the big bands they played in. Record sales were relatively low, and the audience was usually fifty and older. Of the vintage big bands that played music from earlier eras, only the Glenn Miller Orchestra was on tour fifty-two weeks of the year. Happily, the repertoire of this ensemble included the Miller hits as well as pieces that were not as well known.

Stylistically, more and more composer/arrangers were influenced by the current rock trends, electronic instruments and mixed pulses; there was music in straight 4 but variations of pulse, such as alternating 4 and 5 in the same piece as an example. In many bands, there were more instances of created colors versus sections (instead of a trumpet section playing the melody, it might be played by a flugelhorn, piccolo, flute, muted trumpet, trombone, and guitar). As stated earlier, flute had become a required double for saxophone players, and some even doubled oboe, English horn, and bassoon.

This chapter can offer only a sampling of some of the wonderful music that has been created for big band–oriented ensembles since 1980. Bands playing the classic repertoire or that focus on a bandleader since deceased (called "ghost bands") are omitted, except for one or two instances. Thanks to portable video equipment, more and more live performances have been preserved and can be shared.

Rob McConnell was a valve trombonist who was born and raised in Canada. He worked with Clifford Brown and Maynard Ferguson in the United States, but returned to Ontario to become a session musician. He formed the Boss Brass in 1968 as an ensemble of trumpets, French horns, trombones, and rhythm section made up of Toronto's top session players. Initially the ensemble was organized to make recordings of current pop songs for broadcast use; in 1970, a saxophone section was added and the band made commercial albums. Word of the excellence of McConnell's writing and the ensemble itself led to these albums being heard and released in the United States.

What: "T. O." by Rob McConnell
Where: El Mocambo, 464 Spadina Avenue, Toronto, Canada
When: December 1–3, 1980

"T. O." salutes Canadian radio jazz personality Ted O'Reilly, who used this as the theme for his show. McConnell once described this piece as a "blister," probably meaning that it is quite fast ("flag-waver" was an earlier term for a fast, exciting jazz piece). It *is* very fast and exciting, driven by the incredible lead trumpet of Arnie Chycoski and the rhythm section: guitarist Ed Bickert, pianist Jim Dale, bassist Don Thompson, drummer Terry Clarke, and percussionist Marty Morell.

Although this is mostly a straightforward up-tempo track with solos by McConnell accompanied by solo guitar at the beginning (2:02) and tenor saxophonist Rick Wilkins (4:37), McConnell the composer has some surprises for us. After Wilkins's solo (6:07), the band plays a satirical Dixieland section that soon segues into a "free" section (6:36), wherein the musicians play crazily until the tempo returns (6:55).

McConnell then pulls another switch by having the piece end in a slower Basie-type swing section (7:13).

McConnell's ensemble is acknowledged as one of the top big bands of all time. The band rarely toured, as McConnell would not substitute musicians for the ones on the recordings, and they were extremely busy with session work in Toronto (the Thad Jones–Mel Lewis Orchestra was in a similar situation, although there were many subs who were available to travel).

In 1998, McConnell was made an Officer of the Order of Canada, but by 2000, he couldn't manage the costs of maintaining such a large ensemble, and he scaled the band down to a ten piece ensemble, which he led successfully until his death in 2010.

Bob Florence was going to be a concert pianist when he went to Los Angeles City College and became immersed in jazz and big bands. He freelanced after college, writing for Les Brown, Harry James, and a new trombone-playing bandleader named Si Zentner—Florence arranged the Zentner big band recording of "(Up a) Lazy River," which became a huge pop chart hit. After that, Florence was busy writing for bands, singers, and motion pictures throughout the 1970s and 1980s and put together a big band that became legendary for excellent music and the top Los Angeles session players. Such big band veterans as Bob Cooper, Steve Huffsteter, Herbie Harper, and Chauncey Welsch were regulars in this ensemble.

What: "Carmelo's by the Freeway" by Bob Florence
Where: Los Angeles
When: March 3, 1981

Bob Florence's musical range revealed his great love of the traditions of the big band, as well as a talent for thoughtful, expansive ballads. This is an up-tempo, happy piece named for a jazz club. After an introduction, the two A sections are played by straight-muted trumpets and tenor saxes (0:12). The B section is harmonized saxes (0:46), the last A is the same as the previous A's, except with some saxophone embellishment (1:02). The ensemble plays a paraphrase of the melody for a chorus (1:24), then tenor saxophonist Pete Christlieb solos with band background (2:36). Warren Luening solos on trumpet (3:57), and the band comes back roaring (5:12). Florence has a brief solo on piano (6:18), and then the band goes from softly to loudly, repeating the same musical phrases (6:34). The piece ends with another exciting chorus based on the original melody (7:07).

One can hear many different influences in this track—Basie, Buddy Rich, Stan Kenton, Woody Herman—but this is unmistakably Florence's music for the inventiveness of the ideas and the powerful swing of the ensemble. Nick Ceroli's work on drums is unmistakable as well; he was one of the busiest, swingingest, drummers on the West Coast at that time. He passed away much too young in 1985.

Florence's band was yet another ensemble that rarely toured, but Florence himself brought his music to bands all over the world, as well as lecturing and teaching. He died in 2008.

After attending the University of Minnesota and the Eastman School of Music, Maria Schneider was Gil Evans's musical assistant for several years for projects such as Evans's arrangements for Sting and the music for the motion picture *The Color of Money*. She studied with Bob Brookmeyer for five years and formed her own orchestra in 1992. Until the club closed in 1998, the orchestra had a steady Monday night gig at Visiones in Greenwich Village, during which time she made her first recordings and her reputation grew. Appearances at festivals and concerts all over the world have made her an international star as a composer. She was one of the first artists to be part of ArtistShare, in which fans donate money for her to realize recording projects.

Note: Schneider does not allow her recent music to be posted on YouTube, although there's a YouTube link at the end of this book in "Recorded Sources and Further Listening" for a concert of The Hamburg Radio Jazz Orchestra (NDR) big band where she was a guest conductor.

What: "Walking by Flashlight" by Maria Schneider
Where: Avatar Studio C, 441 West 53rd Street, New York
When: August 2014

In 2011, Schneider composed a song cycle for Dawn Upshaw using the poems of Ted Kooser; she says that she envisioned this composition to be an instrumental for her orchestra as well.

Scott Robinson is a woodwind wonder, playing many different and sometimes rare instruments. Here he plays the alto clarinet, the horn slightly larger than the standard clarinet, but smaller than the bass clarinet, which was discussed earlier and is usually doubled by tenor or baritone saxophonists; the alto clarinet is rarely played in the jazz orchestra. Also notice the beautiful bass playing of Jay Anderson under him. Except for Frank Kimbrough's piano solo, it is Robinson's show, and this is a treasurable performance. An interesting color is the accordion played by Gary Versace, which can be heard in the background.

Carla Bley came a long way from being a cigarette girl at Birdland in the late 1950s to being awarded a Guggenheim Fellowship in 1972. Her compositions have been played by George Russell, Jimmy Giuffre, Art Farmer, and pianist Paul Bley, to whom she was married at one time. She organized the Jazz Composers Guild and later wrote and arranged music for Charlie Haden's Liberation Music Orchestra. She was also one of the first artists to start her own record label and music distribution organization.

She organized a big band featuring all-star musicians that has recorded and toured prolifically. Although her music can be quite experimental, much of it is "down-home" funky.

What: "Who Will Rescue You" by Carla Bley
Where: Unknown
When: 1990 (video)

Bley's father was a church choirmaster, and her earliest musical experiences took place in church. Bley later made an album entitled *The Carla Bley Band Goes to Church*, evidence of her continued interest in gospel music. This video comes from a live performance in Europe, and the arrangement shows off the amazing trombonist Gary Valente and the equally outstanding Austrian saxophonist Wolfgang Puschnig. The lead trumpet player is the legendary Lew Soloff.

At this writing, Bley is still at it, playing with small groups and big bands. She has won numerous awards throughout the world and was named a National Endowment for the Arts Jazz Master in 2015.

Cuban composer Arturo "Chico" O'Farrill first came to the United States in 1948, and while continuing his music studies, he wrote for Benny Goodman, Stan Kenton, and Machito and also led his own band (we explored his composition "Undercurrent Blues" in chapter 6). He spent several years in Mexico recording and leading ensembles on television, but he returned to New York in 1965, arranging for Count Basie, the Barry Sisters, and various other acts. For several years, he was out of the jazz and big band world and was the leading writer of jingles for Spanish-language TV commercials seen in New York, Los Angeles, Puerto Rico, and several other countries. After writing arrangements for David Bowie in 1993, he was persuaded to lead his own orchestra in 1995. The ensemble had a regular Sunday night gig at Birdland in 1997, ending in 2011.

What: "Pure Emotion" by Chico O'Farrill
Where: Clinton Recording Studio, 653 10th Avenue, New York
When: February 1995

Although O'Farrill's ensemble played first-class Afro-Cuban music stylings, he showcased music of all types. This piece was originally entitled "Panache" when it was first recorded in November 1966, and except for a brief trombone statement by Gerald Chamberlain (1:12), this is a showcase for alto saxophonist Lenny Hambro, whose first professional job was with Gene Krupa in 1942; he went on to become one of the busiest reed players in New York and also had one of the top music advertising houses, creating jingles for major accounts. After many years in Florida, Hambro returned to participate in O'Farrill's new big band. In November of the same year, Hambro passed away following open heart surgery.

O'Farrill's return to the big band world resulted in three albums and live appearances throughout the world. He passed away in 2001.

When Chico died, his son Arturo took over the ensemble. It is now called the Afro-Latin Jazz Orchestra and has made several award-winning albums. Before that, he established his own reputation playing as a jazz pianist for Carla Bley and Dizzy Gillespie. He reconnected with his Latin roots by meeting with bassist and historian Andy Gonzalez and substituting in Gonzalez's band, Fort Apache. He played in his father's ensemble when it was assembled in 1995 and became its musical director in Chico's final years. In 2010, he took the ensemble to Cuba to headline in the twenty-sixth Havana International Jazz Plaza Festival and has played in Cuba several times.

What: "Guajira Simple" by Arturo O'Farrill
Where: Teatro Mella, Havana, Cuba
When: December 18, 2014 (video)

A live performance from the Jazz Plaza Festival Internacional, this video was produced by O'Farrill; all soloists are identified on the video.

Mario Bauza played saxophone and bass clarinet in Cuba; he came to the United States to play in the Don Azpiazu Orchestra (the ensemble that introduced "The Peanut Vendor" to American audiences). He learned the trumpet in two weeks and played with the Chick Webb and Cab Calloway orchestras (Bauza encouraged Calloway to hire Dizzy Gillespie, who would later seek Bauza's advice when he was looking for a conga player for his 1946 orchestra). Bauza became trumpeter and musical director for his brother-in-law Machito's orchestra, a pioneering ensemble that fused Cuban music and jazz successfully and influenced such future bandleaders as Tito Puente and Tito Rodriguez. The Machito ensemble recorded extensively and toured all over the country. Despite his considerable innovations in bringing two musical cultures together, few knew of Bauza's accomplishments outside the Latin music world.

In 1975, Machito was invited to tour Europe with an octet. Bauza insisted that a smaller ensemble would not fully represent the Machito orchestral sound and did not support the tour. When Machito went anyway, Bauza quit.

When he turned eighty, Bauza assembled an all-star ensemble and celebrated his birthday with a concert at Symphony Space in New York City, becoming a celebrity in his own right. The German Messidor label was quick to record the band, and the ensemble played jazz festivals across the globe.

What: "Chucho" by Paquito D'Rivera
Where: Clinton Recording Studios, 653 10th Avenue, New York
When: December 1991

Legendary Cuban alto saxophonist Paquito D'Rivera wrote this medium-tempo composition and is a guest soloist, and you can hear musical quotes from "Mexican Hat Dance" (2:10) and Tadd Dameron's "Hot House" (2:19). Baritone saxophonist Pablo Calogero has the first solo on the track (0:43), followed by Marcus Persiani soloing on piano (1:22). The legendary percussion section that keeps the steady beat is made up of Juan "Papo" Pepin on congas, Carlos "Patato" Valdez on guiro, Joe Gonzales on bongos, and Bobby Sanabria on drums. The track is also graced by the lead trumpet of Panamanian virtuoso Victor Paz.

Bauza passed away in 1993, and his last album was released posthumously. By the time of his death, the fusion of Cuban music and jazz was second nature in world music, and Bauza was a legend in the musical world.

By 1960, Bill Holman had recorded three albums with his own big band. Over the years he became a very busy arranger for Woody Herman, Terry Gibbs, Count Basie, Harry James, and many solo performers and singers. Thanks to producer and engineer Dayton "Bones" Howe, he arranged for pop groups such as the Association and the Fifth Dimension. In 1975, Holman put together a rehearsal band that is still together as this is written. Holman has received numerous commissions from ensembles in Germany, Holland, Sweden, and Denmark and has recorded several albums, one of which won a Grammy award. Holman has also expanded his musical horizons, studying the music of Igor

Stravinsky, Witold Lutoslawski, Gyorgy Ligeti, and especially Be tok.

What: "Bemsha Swing" by Thelonious Monk and Denzil Best
Where: Oceanway Studios, Sherman Oaks, California
When: February 11 or 12, 1997

Holman's album of the music of Thelonious Monk may be his master-piece; Monk's music is not easy to play, and it is only in the last few years that many improvisers have included his pieces in their repertoire. Holman goes in many directions in his treatment of Monk's unusual music, and yet the listener can still hear the direct, swinging approach Bill uses in his earlier work.

Christian Jacob's piano leads into the main melody (0:06), which is then repeated with a new melodic line underneath, another example of Holman's mastery of counterpoint (0:32). Notice drummer Bob Leath-erbarrow's drums, almost rockishly supporting the ensemble and yet very much right in front of the musical action. Jacob (0:58) and trum-peter Ron Stout solo before new contrapuntal lines are introduced (1:51). Leatherbarrow has a drum solo trading with the ensemble (3:11), and then Bill Perkins solos on alto sax instead of his usual tenor sax (3:58). The melody returns (4:52), and then Holman has brand-new lines against ensemble accents building to a climax (5:22), after which the ensemble simply fades away, playing short riffs.

Tenor saxophonist and composer Bob Mintzer's professional credits include work with Buddy Rich, the Thad Jones–Mel Lewis Orchestra, Tito Puente, James Taylor, Art Blakey's Jazz Messengers, Donald Fag-en, Jaco Pastorius's Word of Mouth Big Band, and many others. A big band that was assembled for a one-time gig at the club Seventh Avenue South (owned by Randy and Michael Brecker) became an ensemble that recorded thirteen albums for the DMP label. Mintzer is also a member of the Yellowjackets, an acclaimed small group that has re-ceived thirteen Grammy nominations and has won numerous polls.

Mintzer taught at the Manhattan School of Music for several years until he relocated to California in 2008, where he is currently on the faculty at the University of Southern California.

**" by Juan Tizol, Duke Ellington, and Irving
y Bob Mintzer
'g, Stuttgart, Germany**
When: December 3, 2014 (video)

Not only does this track feature Mintzer on tenor saxophone, it serves to introduce us to one of the great European ensembles formed for broadcasting, the SWR Big Band. It has been host to some of the greatest composer/arrangers and soloists worldwide and has been nominated for several Grammy awards.

Charles Mingus passed away in 1979, but his widow Sue was determined that his music and legacy live on. She created the Mingus Dynasty band to play his compositions, but that wasn't enough. She went on to create the Mingus Big Band and, in 1999, the Mingus Orchestra; both ensembles have had Monday night residencies at clubs in New York City. They have also recorded several albums and one of them won a Grammy Award.

What: "Jump Monk" by Charles Mingus
Where: Paris
When: July 1994

First written for a small group, the big band played a concert in 1988 where this arrangement was heard.

The Mingus Big Band has always been full of top musicians, some of whom played with Charles himself. Tenor saxophonist John Stubblefield begins this performance over string bass, and instruments are added, creating a chaotic sound. The melody comes in at 0:42, and Kuumba Frank Lacy solos on trombone (1:25). Kenny Drew Jr. plays a piano solo (3:17) entirely alone and out of tempo. He continues in a Latin groove with bass and drums (4:12) as the rest of the band adds background (4:24). The melody returns (5:06) as the groove becomes more intense until several final chords end the piece.

John Fedchock was trombonist and musical director for Woody Herman's "Herd" before he became a freelance musician, performing with T. S. Monk, the Gerry Mulligan Concert Jazz Band, Louie Bellson's Big Band, and several other ensembles on the East and West coasts. He has recorded several albums with his own New York Big Band.

What: "Flintstoned" by John Fedchock ("Flintstone's Theme" by William Hanna and Hoyt Curtin)
Where: New Tier High School, Winnetka, Illinois
When: 2008 (video)

Fedchock's tour de force on the "Flintstone's Theme" was written for Fedchock's own ensemble and has become one of his most popular pieces, yet another score played by students and professionals all over the world.

The melody begins with no rhythm accompaniment, and it may sound strange to you when you hear it. That's because Fedchock is continually moving the key around as the melody continues, creating a feeling of instability. Rhythm comes in (0:22) with a full chorus when alto saxophonist Mark Vinci solos (0:44), followed by trumpeter Scott Wenholdt. Fedchock solos (3:41). Drummer John Riley is featured, first trading with the band, then by himself (5:11). Full band returns (5:52), and the melody is stated for the last time (6:15).

The SpokFrevo Orquesta was the brainchild of Inaldo Cavalcante de Albuquerque (aka Maestro Spok), the ensemble's leader, musical director, and one of the saxophonists in the group. It was his idea to take the Brazilian musical style of Frevo and adapt it to the big band. Originally dating from the nineteenth century, Frevo is a number of musical styles associated with Brazilian Carnival played by large band ensembles; Frevo is supposedly derived from the word *fever*, and the music played at Carnival gets people's feet moving and dancing. Polkas, marches, Brazilian *quadrilha*, and other musical forms are often heard.

The SpokFrevo Orquestra is a standard seventeen-piece big band of saxophones, trumpets, trombones, drums, two percussion, and electric bass; many of the musicians have impressive resumes as sidemen with major jazz artists. Since 2012, it has toured around the world.

What: "Onze de Abril" by Dominguinhas; arranged by Spok
Where: Estudio Carranca, Recife, Brazil
When: 2014

Please note: the YouTube link has the entire album *Ninho de Vespra* (Wasp's Nest). The track under discussion is the first one.

This music is clearly filled with fire and swing. Guest Paulo Sergio Santos solos on clarinet (he has played with Peter Gabriel and Phillip Glass) (0:52), as do Renato Bandeira on guitar (1:58) and Spok on soprano saxophone (2:49). The sheer virtuosity of all of these musicians playing this difficult music sounding as one person is breathtaking.

The SpokFrevo Orquestra is another stunning example of a musician reimagining native folk music as material for a swinging, exciting big band played by musicians steeped in the tradition. As of this writing, the ensemble continues to draw bigger and bigger audiences of all age groups.

Darcy James Argue graduated from McGill University in 1998 and came to the United States to study with Bob Brookmeyer at the New England Conservatory. Moving to Brooklyn, New York, in 2003, he attended the BMI Jazz Composers Workshop. His ensemble is named Darcy James Argue's Secret Society and has been performing at clubs and festivals. His recordings have been nominated for numerous awards and have been cited as among the best albums of the year in numerous polls.

What: "Obsidian Flow" by Darcy James Argue
Where: The Kennedy Center, Washington, D.C.
When: January 5, 2011 (video)

This video was uploaded by the composer himself from a live concert; it is a feature for alto saxophonist David DeJesus. Argue is a master of orchestration: the video allows us to actually see the different instrumental combinations (for example, at the beginning, clarinets, baritone sax, flugelhorn, two trumpets in cup mutes, two trumpets in Harmon mutes [Argue shifts the colors of the trumpet section so that three trumpets play flugelhorn at one point], trombones in bucket mutes, guitar, piano, bass, drums; also note that the guitar is used both as a melodic instrument and a rhythm instrument, a trend that began in the 1970s). Color groupings move from clarinets and trombones to flugelhorns and muted trumpets as an example. Watch Argue as he conducts 3 and sometimes 2, creating a free rhythmic flow. The piece builds to a powerful climax.

Argue continues to create interesting and challenging music and is a major influence in the big band world of today.

Tom Kubis is one of the finest examples of the traditional big band writer who brings new elements to his music. He studied composition at Long Beach State and soon became a mainstay in the Hollywood musical scene as a saxophonist and composer/arranger. Composer, writer, and talk show host Steve Allen hired Kubis as his musical director for several years. It's safe to say that every big band in the world probably has at least one Kubis arrangement in its book, and many have been recorded hundreds of times by ensembles both educational and professional.

What: "Bill Bailey, Won't You Please Come Home" by Hughie Cannon; arranged by Tom Kubis
Where: Don the Beachcomber's, Huntington Beach, California
When: August 25, 2014 (video)

This was the closer of the evening at this popular restaurant and club where the Kubis band is regularly featured as of this writing. The soloists are identified in the text accompanying the video and are also announced at the end of the performance. This is unadulterated swinging fun for eleven solid minutes. Note how the ensemble plays a tricky syncopated passage without the support of the rhythm section (2:37) building the tension that explodes when the rhythm comes back (3:09).

Gordon Goodwin is much in demand as a composer/arranger in the film world, and he also leads his own big band and small group. He has thirteen Grammy nominations and has won one Grammy and three

Emmy awards. He has worked with Ray Charles, Natalie Cole, John Williams, David Foster, Sarah Vaughan, Mel Torme, and many others. He has conducted the Atlanta, Dallas, Utah, Seattle, Toronto, and London symphony orchestras.

What: "Hunting Wabbits" by Gordon Goodwin
Where: Hollywood
When: 2003

Typical of how eclectic big band music continues to be in the 2010s, this track begins as if it is a concert piece for five saxophones played entirely straight. Trombones take over (0:47), leading to a full band explosion (1:26). The band starts swinging (2:18), and as trombonist Andy Martin solos, we realize that the introduction has been one big buildup to a minor blues. Tenor saxophonist Brian Scanlon takes over the solo space (3:13). After a short bongo solo (4:07), the band begins a slow build with layer upon layer added as the volume gets louder and louder. The band and the drums trade phrases (5:19), and then there's a return of the concert feel (5:40) until the piece ends quietly.

Trumpet and flugelhorn artist Steve Huffsteter has played and soloed with bands led by Stan Kenton, Gerald Wilson, Clare Fischer, Mike Barone, Bob Florence, Tom Talbert, Louis Bellson, and the Toshiko Akiyoshi–Lew Tabackin ensemble. Although Huffsteter had been writing music throughout his playing career, he rarely wrote for big bands due to the sheer amount of work of writing out a score and then copying the parts himself. When he bought a computer and learned how to write scores and parts digitally, it made writing the music far easier for him. In his words, "I became whole."

What: "Circles" by Steve Huffsteter
Where: Zipper Concert Hall (Colburn School for Performing Arts), Los Angeles
When: April 17, 2003 (video)

The bass and drums (using brushes instead of sticks) start off this re-laxed, fast-tempo piece that is made up of short phrases that are intro-duced and evolve playing against each other, leading to the melody, which is derived from all of these phrases. Solos are by Huffsteter (1:17), tenor saxophonist Jerry Pinter (2:31), acoustic guitarist Jamie Findley (3:45), and pianist Mark Massey (4:57). Full ensemble returns, consisting of all these phrases together, then the melody returns as the ensemble plays softer and softer until we are back to the bass and drums to end the piece.

Huffsteter is another writer who does not write by section, prefer-ring to mix orchestral colors (soprano sax, flugelhorn, and trombone make up one color as an example). He also derives new colors by having the trumpet section split between trumpets and flugelhorns.

The last three compositions are larger works that are presented in their entirety.

Kenny Wheeler and his friend, lyricist, writer, and singer Gene Lees, agreed that if they stayed in Canada, they would not be heard or recognized in their native country. In 1952, they decided to go to Eng-land where they felt there were greater opportunities for their talents. Lees changed his mind at the last minute, but Wheeler made the trip. By the latter part of the decade, he was well established as a trumpet/flugelhorn soloist of considerable ability. He was a soloist with Johnny Dankworth's big band, and Dankworth lent him his band for Wheeler's first album as a big band composer, *Windmill Tilter*, considered one of the finest big band albums of the 1960s. Wheeler also became part of the British free jazz scene, playing with Anthony Braxton from 1971 through 1976. He led various small groups as well as big bands through-out Europe and made many important recordings. He died in 2014.

What: "The Sweet Time Suite" by Kenny Wheeler
Where: London
When: January 1990

This is one of Wheeler's most impressive achievements and gives us an opportunity to listen to his subtle yet powerful sounds. Note that he uses the soprano voice of Norma Winstone to sing the melody along with the trumpet and alto saxophone.

Kamasi Washington studied music in Los Angeles and played with Kenny Burrell, Wayne Shorter, Herbie Hancock, and Gerald Wilson, among many others. He has also performed with Lauryn Hill, Snoop Dogg, Nas, and Kendrick Lamar. In 2015, he composed and recorded a work that filled three CDs entitled *The Epic*, which garnered wide critical acclaim and became a best-selling album.

What: *The Epic* by Kamasi Washington
Where: Regent Theater, Los Angeles
When: August 2015

Linked here is the performance given at the official record release party for the album. The various sections of this work are scored for anything from small group, big band and choir, and large jazz orchestra and choir. This composition shows how ambitious composer/arrangers had become in the twenty-first century, as this is indeed a work of epic proportions, in which the parts are as impressive as the work in its entirety.

Jazz at Lincoln Center and the orchestra musical directed by Wynton Marsalis perform repertoire ranging from Louis Armstrong to contemporary music. In 2014, composer and reed player Ted Nash composed a large work entitled *The Presidential Suite*, mixing speeches with musical composition for the jazz orchestra. The album won two Grammy awards.

What: *The Presidential Suite: Eight Variations on Freedom* **by Ted Nash**
Where: Rose Theater, Columbus Circle, New York
When: January 18, 2014

This is a live concert of the work. Charles S. Dutton speaks the words of several world leaders, including John F. Kennedy, Winston Churchill, Jawaharlal Nehru, Franklin D. Roosevelt, and Nelson Mandela. In Nash's words, the speeches "use the intonation of the voice to form the thematic material, and the spirit and message to shape the intensity of the arrangements."

The big band started out as an ensemble for dancing and has continued to evolve as an art form. For many years it was difficult to obtain the music created for the bands, but by the 1970s, transcribers began to re-create the classics of the repertoire, and in the years following, many of the original libraries of bands known and unknown were donated to libraries, universities, the Smithsonian Institution, and the Library of Congress. New, edited, and corrected editions of this music began to be published (I was a pioneering editor in this endeavor), and ensembles now have a sizable repertoire of performance materials from Fletcher Henderson to the present. The music and the bands are subjects of masters and doctoral theses and courses in colleges. Even though the ensemble is no longer the focus of popular music the way it once was, it is as visible and as audible as ever.

SUGGESTED READINGS AND PERSONAL INTERVIEWS

This book benefitted from a great deal of first- and secondhand source material, as well as modern in-depth research and personal interviews with the musicians who played in the bands covered. These interviews began back in the 1960s and continue to the present day.

This list is an invitation for further exploration and research into a wonderful musical world.

BOOKS

Abbott, Lynn, and Doug Seroff. *Out of Sight: The Rise of African American Popular Music, 1889–1895*. Jackson: University Press of Mississippi, 2002.
———. *Ragged but Right: Black Traveling Shows, "Coon Songs," & the Dark Pathway to Blues and Jazz*. Jackson: University Press of Mississippi, 2007.
Acosta, Leonardo. *Cubano Be Cubano Bop: One Hundred Years of Jazz in Cuba*. Translated by David S. Whitesell. Washington, DC: Smithsonian Books, 2003.
Badger, Reid. *A Life in Ragtime: A Biography of James Reese Europe*. New York: Oxford University Press, 1995.
Berresford, Mark. *That's Got 'Em! The Life and Music of Wilbur C. Sweatman*. Jackson: University Press of Mississippi, 2010.
Charters, Samuel. *A Trumpet around the Corner: The Story of New Orleans Jazz*. Jackson: University Press of Mississippi, 2008.
Determeyer, Eddy. *Rhythm Is Our Business: Jimmie Lunceford and the Harlem Express*. Ann Arbor: University of Michigan Press, 2006.
Firestone, Ross. *Swing, Swing, Swing: The Life & Times of Benny Goodman*. New York: W. W. Norton, 1993.
Gitler, Ira. *Jazz Masters of the 40's*. New York: Macmillan, 1966.
Harris, Steven. *The Kenton Kronicles*. Pasadena, CA: Dynaflow Publications, 2000.
Kenney, William Howland. *Chicago Jazz: A Cultural History, 1904–1930*. New York: Oxford University Press, 1993.

Kirchner, Bill, ed. *The Oxford Companion to Jazz*. New York: Oxford University Press, 2005.

Kubick, Gerhard. *Africa and the Blues*. Jackson: University Press of Mississippi, 1999.

Lange, Arthur. *Arranging for the Modern Dance Orchestra*. New York: Arthur Lange, 1926.

Lotz, Rainer E. "Black Music Prior to the First World War—American Origins and German Perspectives." In *Cross the Water Blues*, ed. Neal A. Wynn. Jackson: University Press of Mississippi, 2007.

Magee, Jeffrey. *The Uncrowned King of Swing: Fletcher Henderson and Big Band Jazz*. New York: Oxford University Press, 2005.

Robertson, David. *W. C. Handy: The Life and Times of the Man Who Made the Blues*. New York: Alfred A. Knopf, 2009.

Rose, Frank. *The Agency: William Morris and the Hidden History of Show Business*. New York: HarperCollins, 1995.

Sparke, Michael. *Stan Kenton: This Is an Orchestra!* Denton: University of North Texas Press, 2010.

Watkins, Clifford Edward. *Showman: The Life and Music of Perry George Lowery*. Jackson: University Press of Mississippi, 2003.

PERSONAL INTERVIEWS

Those listed below are musicians and/or historians. In many cases they created some of the music discussed here, and were friends with or have had contact with those who created the music. They supplied much-needed information and recordings; many of them I consider my friends.

Desne Villepigue Ahlers (Paul Villepigue)

Johnny Amoroso (Tommy Dorsey)

Tino Barzie (Dorsey Brothers)

Rick Benjamin

Ed Berger (Benny Carter)

Benny Carter

Paul Combs (Tadd Dameron)

Bob Curnow (Stan Kenton, Maynard Ferguson)

Blossom Dearie (Woody Herman)

Clem DeRosa

George Duvivier (Jimmie Lunceford)

Anthony Esposito (Tito Puente)

Miles Evans (Gil Evans)

Robert Farnon (Ted Heath, Geraldo)

Clare Fischer

Michael Fitzgerald

Frank Foster (Count Basie)

Herb Geller

Vince Giordano
Jerry Graff (Dorsey Brothers)
Eddie Harvey (John Dankworth)
Neal Hefti (Woody Herman, Harry James)
Tad Hershhorn
Ray Hoffman
Bill Holman (Stan Kenton, Woody Herman)
Andrew Homzy (Duke Ellington, Charles Mingus)
Ron Hutchinson
Dick Hyman
Budd Johnson (Earl Hines, Billy Eckstine, Count Basie, Gil Evans)
Bill Kirchner
James T. Maher
Johnny Mandel (Count Basie, Boyd Raeburn, Buddy Rich)
Sue Mingus (Charles Mingus)
Dan Morgenstern
Sy Oliver (Jimmie Lunceford, Tommy Dorsey)
Vincent Pelote
Sy "Red" Press (Tommy Dorsey)
Jerome Richardson (Thad Jones, Mel Lewis)
Nelson Riddle (Charlie Spivak, Tommy Dorsey)
Lynn Roberts (Charlie Spivak, Dorsey Brothers, Harry James)
Ron Roullier (Ted Heath)
Pete Rugolo
Loren Schoenberg
Chris Sheridan (Count Basie)
Derek Smith (John Dankworth)
Marvin Stamm (Stan Kenton)
Richard Sudhalter (Paul Whiteman, Benny Goodman, Bix Beider-
    becke)
Terry Teachout
Walter Van de Leur (Billy Strayhorn)
Ed Wasserman (Benny Goodman)
Paul Weston (Tommy Dorsey)
Ernie Wilkins (Count Basie, Tommy Dorsey)
Joe Williams (Count Basie)

RECORDED SOURCES AND FURTHER LISTENING

RECORDED SOURCES

This section is presented so that readers can access the YouTube recordings and videos discussed in this book, and it also lists additional performances so that readers can continue to explore the worlds of jazz and the big band with some guidance. So that readers can navigate these additional recordings, chapter listings provide historical context for these bands. This list is only the tip of the iceberg with regard to a lot of amazing music, but it's a start.

A disclaimer: there's a lot of great music that is simply not available on YouTube (some titles I wanted to include are not found there), so I have listed titles that may be found elsewhere. Spotify is an excellent first source to check.

Recordings are listed by band leader rather than composer.

The YouTube videos for the Recorded Sources and Further Listening lists have been assembled into special playlists accessible at the Rowman & Littlefield Music Channel: www.youtube.com/channel/UCAlMT_8diMruPuGy39xCHHQ. The recordings listed here are numbered to correspond to the YouTube playlists.

Chapter 1

1. Europe—"Memphis Blues"

2. Europe—"St. Louis Blues"

3. Hickman—"The Hesitating Blues"

Chapter 2

4. Jones—"Wabash Blues"

5. Whiteman—"Changes"

6. Whiteman—"Changes" alternate take

7. Whiteman—"Lonely Melody"

8. Henderson—"Copenhagen"

9. Henderson—"Shanghai Shuffle" (Pathe)

10. Henderson—"Shanghai Shuffle" (Vocalion)

11. Henderson—"Blazin'"

12. Ellington—"The Mooche" (OKeh)

13. Ellington—"The Mooche" (Brunswick)

14. Ellington—"Cotton Club Stomp"

15. Goldkette—"My Pretty Girl"

16. Goldkette—"Clementine"

17. Pollack—"Singapore Sorrows"

18. Russell—"Jersey Lightning"

19. McKinney's Cotton Pickers—"Wherever There's a Will, Baby"

20. Ambrose—"Do Something"

21. Elizalde—"Singapore Sorrows"

Chapter 3

22. Moten—"Moten Swing"

23. Hughes—"Firebird"

24. Redman—"Chant of the Weed"

25. Ellington—"Ring Dem Bells"

26. Ellington—"Sophisticated Lady"

27. Ellington—"Stompy Jones"

28. Ellington—"Solitude"

29. Casa Loma—"Black Jazz"

30. Henderson—"Queer Notions"

31. Henderson—"Shanghai Shuffle"

32. Trent—"Clementine"

33. Hines—"Rosetta"

Chapter 4

34. Goodman—"Ridin' High"
35. Goodman—"Goodnight My Love" (Fitzgerald)
36. Goodman—"Goodnight My Love" (Hunt)
37. Goodman—"Just Like Taking Candy from a Baby"
38. Goodman—"Solo Flight"
39. Goodman—"Solo Flight" alternate take
40. Goodman—"Why Don't You Do Right?"
41. "Stage Door Canteen" clip
42. Dorsey—"Stop, Look and Listen"
43. Shaw—"Cream Puff"
44. Shaw—"Begin the Beguine"
45. Shaw—"Just Kiddin' Around"
46. Lunceford—"My Blue Heaven"
47. Lunceford—"Baby, Won't You Please Come Home?"
48. Ellington—"Ko-Ko"
49. Ellington—"Jack the Bear"
50. Ellington—"Chelsea Bridge"
51. Webb—"Undecided"
52. Basie—"Time Out"
53. Basie—"Broadway"
54. Kirk—"Walkin' and Swingin'"
55. Norvo—"Smoke Dreams"
56. Miller—"In the Mood" (original version)
57. Miller—"In the Mood" (final version)
58. Miller—"Song of the Volga Boatman"
59. McShann—"Hootie Blues"
60. Leonard—"Rock and Ride"
61. Calloway—"Pickin' the Cabbage"
62. Carter—"Sleep"

Chapter 5

63. Miller AEF Band—"In the Mood"
64. Donahue Navy Band—"Convoy"
65. Barnet—"Skyliner"
66. Eckstine—"Air Mail Special"

67. Kenton—"And Her Tears Flowed Like Wine"
68. Kenton—"And Her Tears Flowed Like Wine" alternate take
69. Dorsey—"Opus No. 1"
70. Basie—"Rambo"
71. Ellington—"Overture to a Jam Session"
72. Shaw—"Summertime"
73. Herman—"Happiness Is a Thing Called Joe"
74. Herman—"Sidewalks of Cuba"
75. McKinley—"Hangover Square"
76. Rich—"Dateless Brown"
77. Gillespie—"Our Delight"
78. Gillespie—"One Bass Hit"
79. Raeburn—"Dalvatore Sally"
80. Raeburn—"There's No You"

Chapter 6

81. Thornhill—"Robbins' Nest"
82. Thornhill—"Yardbird Suite (What Price Love)"
83. Gillespie—"Manteca"
84. Herman—"The Goof and I"
85. Herman—"Early Autumn"
86. Hampton—"Mingus Fingers"
87. Basie—"Normania (Blee Blop Blues)"
88. Goodman—"Undercurrent Blues"
89. Wilson—"Dissonance in Blues"
90. Brown—"I've Got My Love to Keep Me Warm"
91. Machito—"Tanga"
92. Kenton—"Machito"
93. Ellington—"I Like the Sunrise"
94. Jackson—"Father Knickerbopper"
95. Heath—"Father Knickerbopper"
96. Barnet—"Lonely Street"

Chapter 7

97. Sauter–Finegan—"Solo for Joe"
98. Brown—"Montoona Clipper"

99. Thornhill—"Jeru"
100. Ellington—"Satin Doll"
101. May—"The Sheik of Araby"
102. Rogers—"Hot Blood" ("The Wild One")
103. Rogers—"Topsy"
104. Puente—"Live a Little"
105. Machito—"Cannonology"
106. Machito—"Blues a la Machito"
107. Gillespie—"Dizzy's Business"
108. Basie—"April in Paris"
109. Basie—"Blues in Frankie's Flat"
110. Basie—"Cute"
111. Kenton—"Stompin' at the Savoy"
112. Kenton—"Recurerdos (Reminiscences)"
113. Pettiford—"Smoke Signal"
114. Richards—"Walk Softly"
115. Evans–Davis—"Springsville"
116. Russell—"Manhattan"
117. Dankworth—"Experiments with Mice"
118. Arnold—"The Midnight Sun Will Never Set"

Chapter 8

119. Mulligan—"All about Rosie"
120. Ferguson—"Sometimes I Feel Like a Motherless Child"
121. James—"The Jazz Connoisseur"
122. Jones—"Meet B. B."
123. Jones–Lewis—"Don't Get Sassy"
124. Jones–Lewis—"Us"
125. Wilson—"Viva Tirado"
126. Kenton—"Tonight"
127. Ellis—"Indian Lady"
128. Fischer—"Miles Behind"
129. McFarland—"Manha de Carnaval (Morning of Carnaval)"
130. Evans—"Up from the Skies"
131. Rich—"New Blues"
132. Pearson—"New Girl"
133. Clarke–Boland—"Griff's Groove"

134. Sun Ra—"King Porter Stomp"
135. Akiyoshi–Tabackin—"Henpecked Old Man"
136. Ellington—"Blood Count"
137. Ellington—"Satin Doll"
138. McGregor—"The Bride"
139. Mingus—"Don't Be Afraid, the Clown's Afraid Too"
140. Sebesky—"Free As a Bird"

Chapter 9

141. McConnell—"T. O."
142. Florence—"Carmelo's by the Freeway"
143. Bley—"Who Will Rescue You?"
144. C. O'Farrill—"Pure Emotion"
145. A. O'Farrill—"Guajira Simple"
146. Bauza—"Chucho"
147. Holman—"Bemsha Swing"
148. Mintzer—"Caravan"
149. Mingus Big Band—"Jump Monk"
150. Fedchock—"Flintstoned"
151. SpokFrevo—"Onze de Abril"
152. Argue—"Obsidian Flow"
153. Kubis—"Bill Bailey"
154. Goodwin—"Hunting Wabbits"
155. Huffsteter—"Circles"
156. Wheeler—"The Sweet Time Suite"
157. Washington—"The Epic"
158. Nash (LCJO)—"The Presidential Suite: Eight Variations on Freedom"

FOR FURTHER LISTENING

The list below is an open invitation to the reader to further investigate and discover more music and more about big bands from the 1920s through press time.

Along with lists of tracks by bandleaders discussed in the text, there are others whose music should be heard as well. These links direct you to recordings, television appearances, and even live concerts. By accessing the supplied links, readers can also find other links for more music. I wish you a wonderful journey!

Ambrose, Bert

1. "Limehouse Blues" (chapter 4)
2. "Swing Low, Sweet Clarinet" (chapter 6)

Armstrong, Louis

3. "Stardust" (chapter 3)
4. "I Got Rhythm" (chapter 3)
5. "Basin Street Blues" (chapter 3)
6. "When It's Sleepy Time Down South" (chapter 3)
7. "I've Got the World on a String" (chapter 3)

Auld, George

8. "In the Middle" (chapter 5)
9. "Co-pilot" (chapter 5)
10. "A Hundred Years from Today" (chapter 5)
11. "Air Mail Special" (chapter 5)

Barnet, Charlie

12. "Pompton Turnpike" (chapter 4)
13. "Washington Whirligig" (chapter 5)
14. "Charlie's Other Aunt" (chapter 6)

Basie, William (Count)

15. "Topsy" (chapter 4)
16. "John's Idea" (chapter 4)
17. "Cherokee" (chapter 4)
18. "Avenue C" (chapter 4)
19. "Stay on It" (chapter 5)

20. "The Atomic Mr. Basie"—complete album (chapter 7)
21. "Moten Swing" (chapter 7)
22. "Basie Straight Ahead" (chapter 8)

Beneke, Tex, and the Glenn Miller Orchestra

23. "Hey-Ba-Ba-Re-Bop" (chapter 5)

Berigan, Bunny

24. "I Can't Get Started" (chapter 4)
25. "The Prisoner's Song" (chapter 4)

Brown, Les

26. "Bizet Has His Day" (chapter 4)
27. "Leap Frog" (chapter 5)
28. "Come to Baby Do" (chapter 5)
29. "Night Blooming Jazzman" (chapter 7)

Burke, Sonny

30. "What, Where and When" (chapter 7)
31. "Mambo Jambo" (chapter 7)

Butterfield, Billy

32. "Singin' the Blues" (chapter 7)

Calloway, Cab

33. "Jumpin' Jive" (chapter 4)
34. "Foo Little Ballyhoo" (chapter 5)

Carter, Benny

35. "Lonesome Nights" (chapter 3)

Casa Loma

36. "Maniac's Ball" (chapter 3)

Crosby, Bob

37. "South Rampart Street Parade" (chapter 4)
38. "What's New?" (chapter 4)

Dankworth, John

39. "Just in Time" (chapter 8)
40. "Two-Piece Flower" (chapter 8)

Donahue, Sam

41. "C Jam Blues" (chapter 5)
42. "Deep Night/I Found a New Baby" (chapter 5)

Dorsey Brothers

43. "By Heck" (chapter 3)
44. "Sentimental Me" (chapter 7)

Dorsey, Jimmy

45. "Sunset Strip" (chapter 5)

Dorsey, Tommy

46. "Bingo, Bango, Boffo" (chapter 5)
47. "Hollywood Hat" (chapter 5)
48. "The Continental" (chapter 6)

Eckstine, Billy

49. "Rhythm in a Riff" (chapter 5)

50. "Oo Bop Sh'bam" (chapter 5)

Ellington, Duke

51. "Warm Valley" (chapter 4)
52. "C Jam Blues" (chapter 4)
53. "Reminiscing in Tempo" (chapter 6)
54. "Black" (from *Black, Brown and Beige*) (chapter 5)
55. "Harlem" (chapter 7)
56. "Diminuendo and Crescendo in Blue" (chapter 7)

Ellis, Don

57. "Bulgarian Bulge" (chapter 8)

Ferguson, Maynard

58. "Geller's Cellar" (chapter 7)
59. "Oleo" (chapter 8)
60. "Birdland" (chapter 8)

Fisher, Clare

61. "Lennie's Pennies" (chapter 8)
62. "Theirs' Tears" (chapter 8)

Gillespie, Dizzy

63. "Salt Peanuts" (chapter 5)
64. "Jessica's Day" (chapter 7)
65. "Tour de Force" (chapter 7)

Goodman, Benny

66. "Take My Word" (chapter 3)
67. "Sing, Sing, Sing" (chapter 4)
68. "Benny Rides Again" (chapter 4)

69. "Scarecrow" (chapter 4)
70. "Oh, Baby" (chapter 5)
71. "Fontainebleau" (chapter 8)

Hampton, Lionel

72. "Flying Home" (chapter 5)
73. "Goldwyn Stomp" (chapter 6)

Hawkins, Erskine

74. "Tuxedo Junction" (chapter 4)
75. "After Hours" (chapter 4)

Heath, Ted

76. "Lady Bird" (chapter 6)
77. "Strike up the Band" (chapter 7)
78. "The Champ" (chapter 7)
79. "Eloquence" (chapter 7)

Henderson, Fletcher

80. "How Come You Do Me Like You Do?" (chapter 2)
81. "Sugarfoot Stomp" (chapter 2)
82. "Henderson Stomp" (chapter 2)
83. "Whiteman Stomp" (chapter 2)
84. "Down South Camp Meeting" (chapter 3)
85. "Christopher Columbus" (chapter 4)
86. "Shoe Shine Boy" (chapter 4)

Herman, Woody

87. "Crying Sands" (chapter 5)
88. "Everywhere" (chapter 5)
89. "Lady McGowan's Dream" (chapter 5)
90. "Four Brothers" (chapter 6)

Hines, Earl

91. "Madhouse" (chapter 3)
92. "Grand Terrace Shuffle" (chapter 4)
93. "Swingin' on C" (chapter 4)
94. "Stormy Monday Blues" (chapter 5)
95. "Scoops Carry's Merry (Fatha's Idea)" (chapter 5)

James, Harry

96. "Blues for Sale" (chapter 7)
97. "Moten Swing" (chapter 7)

Jenney, Jack

98. "Stardust" (chapter 4)

Jones, Quincy

99. "Stockholm Sweetnin'" (chapter 7)
100. "Quintessence" (chapter 8)
101. "Portrait Robot" (chapter 8)
102. "Killer Joe" (chapter 9)

Kenton, Stan

103. "Fascinating Rhythm" (chapter 7)
104. "Artemis and Apollo" (chapter 8)
105. "Here's That Rainy Day" (chapter 8)
106. "Bogota" (chapter 8)

Krupa, Gene

107. "Thanks for the Boogie Ride" (chapter 4)
108. "Disc Jockey Jump" (chapter 5)

Leonard, Harlan

109. "A la Bridges" (chapter 4)
110. "Dameron Stomp" (chapter 4)

Lunceford, Jimmie

111. Jimmie Lunceford and his Orchestra (video) (chapter 4)
112. "Hi Spook" (chapter 4)
113. "Yard Dog Mazurka" (chapter 4)

Machito (Mario Grillo)

114. "The Afro-Cuban Suite" (chapter 6)
115. "Barbarabatiri" (chapter 6)
116. "Mambo a la Savoy" (chapter 7)
117. "Sambia" (chapter 7)

May, Billy

118. "All of Me" (chapter 7)
119. "Easy Street" (chapter 7)
120. "The Late Late Show" (chapter 8)

McKinley, Ray

121. "Borderline" (chapter 5)
122. "Tumblebug" (chapter 5)

McKinney's Cotton Pickers

123. "Plain Dirt" (chapter 2)
124. "Gee Baby, Ain't I Good to You?" (chapter 2)

Miller, Glenn

125. "Solid As a Stonewall, Jackson" (chapter 4)

126. "A String of Pearls" (chapter 4)
127. "Blues in the Night" (chapter 4)

Mingus, Charles

128. "The 'I' of Hurricane Sue" (chapter 8)

Moten, Bennie

129. "Toby" (chapter 3)
130. "Milenburg Joys" (chapter 3)

Mulligan, Gerry

131. "Motel" (chapter 7)
132. "Django's Castle (Manoir de mes reves)" (chapter 8)
133. "Israel" (chapter 8)

Nichols, Red

134. "Indiana" (chapter 2)
135. "On Revival Day" Part 1 (chapter 3)
136. "On Revival Day" Part 2 (chapter 3)

Norvo, Red

137. "A Porter's Love Song to a Chambermaid" (chapter 4)
138. "Remember" (chapter 4)
139. "Russian Lullaby" (chapter 4)
140. "Please Be Kind" (chapter 4)

Puente, Tito

141. "Birdland after Dark" (chapter 7)
142. "Mambo Beat" (chapter 7)
143. "Take Five" (chapter 9)

Raeburn, Boyd

144. "A Night in Tunisia" (chapter 5)
145. "Yerxa" (chapter 5)
146. "Picnic in the Wintertime" (chapter 5)

Redman, Don

147. "Nagasaki" (chapter 3)
148. "Doin' the New Low-Down" (chapter 3)

Rich, Buddy

149. "Song of the Islands" (chapter 7)
150. "Channel One Suite" (chapter 8)
151. "West Side Story Medley" (chapter 8)

Rogers, Shorty

152. "Saturnian Sleigh Ride" (chapter 7)
153. "Martian's Lullaby" (chapter 7)

Sauter-Finegan

154. "Concerto in F" (chapter 7)
155. "Moonlight on the Ganges" (chapter 8)
156. "Child's Play" (chapter 7)
157. "Little Brown Jug" (chapter 7)

Schneider, Maria

158. NDR Big Band Concert (chapter 9)

Shaw, Artie

159. "Stardust" (chapter 4)
160. "St. James Infirmary" (chapter 4)

161. "Lady Day" (chapter 5)
162. "Innuendo" (chapter 6)

Spivak, Charlie

163. "Charlie Horse" (chapter 4)

Thornhill, Claude

164. "Arab Dance" (chapter 4)
165. "Anthropology" (chapter 5)
166. "Donna Lee" (chapter 5)

Webb, Chick

167. "Stompin' at the Savoy" (chapter 3)
168. "Blue Lou" (chapter 3)
169. "Harlem Congo" (chapter 3)

Whiteman, Paul

170. "Whiteman Stomp" (chapter 2)
171. "Travelin' Light" (chapter 4)

Wills, Bob

172. "Big Beaver" (chapter 4)

Wilson, Gerald

173. "Blues for Yna Yna" (chapter 8)
174. "Nancy Jo" (chapter 8)
175. "Light My Fire" (chapter 8)

DO YOU WANT TO PLAY THIS MUSIC?

Many of the compositions and arrangements discussed in this volume are available in editions for sale. Visit www.ejazzlines.com.

TEACHER GUIDE AVAILABLE

For instructors of high school and college music and history courses (from Bachelors to Doctoral levels), there is a Teacher Guide available, which includes:

- Lesson Plans
- Additional study and listening materials
- Suggested activities for homework and research papers
- Questions for discussion

This guide can be used for both classroom and online courses.
    Please contact the author at jeffsultanof@ejazzlines.com.

NAME INDEX

SONG INDEX

ABOUT THE AUTHOR

Jeff Sultanof is a composer, arranger, conductor, historian, editor, and teacher. He edited the textbook *Arranged by Nelson Riddle* as editorial director of Warner Bros. Publications, where he also edited facsimile editions of the orchestral works of George Gershwin. Sultanof was one of the first editors of jazz and big band ensemble music utilizing original scores and parts, notably the repertoire of the Miles Davis 1949–1950 nonet. He has lectured on American music in the United States and England and has published articles and reviews in the *Journal of Jazz Studies*, *Jazz Perspectives*, jazz.com, and the blogs Do the Math and Rifftides. His compositions and arrangements are published by Walrus Music.

CPSIA information can be obtained
at www.ICGtesting.com
Printed in the USA
BVOW08*2128271017
498665BV00002B/2/P